1001
WOODWORKING
HINTS
AND TIPS

Future
BOOKS

First published in 1994 by

Future Books

A division of Future Publishing Limited

30 Monmouth Street, Bath BA1 2BW

Copyright © Future Publishing 1994

Designed by Maria Bowers.

Illustrations by John Lander

Edited by Alison Stewart

A catalogue record of this book is available from The British Library

ISBN: 1 85981 075 6

Printed and bound in the UK by Ebenezer Baylis Ltd

We take great care to ensure that what we print is accurate, but
we cannot accept liability for any mistakes or misprints.

CONTENTS

Introduction
by Nick Gibbs, Editor of *Good Woodworking* Magazine

When I read a magazine, be it for woodworkers or anyone else, I turn swiftly to the pages of tips. I measure the success of a publication by the number of hints I've never considered but would love to claim as my own. The endless stream of new, and often lateral, ideas amazes me. So the thought of a collection of *Good Woodworking* experts combining to produce a book of their own tips seems too good to be true.

Digging into this fascinating book, I loved the idea of holding leather or cork facings on an engineer's vice with fridge magnets, and of making a special "mouse" for levelling chair or table legs. I've even discovered a way of demagnetising tools to rid them of all the filings and little screws they can't help picking up.

The full extremes of woodworking are represented. For example, you can find out how to use springy Go Bars for holding items between the bench and the ceiling; in contrast, I had never thought of the restorer's trick of using old upholstery springs for fixing repairs.

I am very grateful to our guest contributor, Ray Key, for his turning tip on grinding wheels, as I'm currently looking for new ones and welcome his advice. The section on designing furniture is equally informative. I will certainly be taking up the idea of using a mirror to judge your own work more critically, and can understand the hint to take a short break from a tricky problem: "the solution suddenly presents itself as crystal clear".

And what of my tip, I hear you ask. Well, I recommend you buy this book, and, of course, *Good Woodworking* magazine!

TIMBER

Project Requirements
The choice of timber for a project is determined by the characteristics of the timber (must it be light, strong, weather resistant, etc?); the final environment (must it sit alongside pieces made from oak or mahogany?); your workshop equipment (heavy hardwood is very demanding); and your expertise. Start with good quality softwood. Graduate to oak.

The Timberyard

YARD SPECIALITY
Find out about the timberyards in your area. Some will specialise in imported timber, some in home-grown and others in softwood. Many will have a bit of everything but only their speciality is likely to be competitively priced.

INSPECTION/SELECTION
Ask if you will be permitted to sift through and select your own boards. Some yards don't mind at all but others insist you take the boards as they come. Larger companies might only sell whole trees! Will you be surcharged for choosing highly figured boards? In a softwood yard or at a builders merchant you may be accompanied by a sales assistant: be quick to judge the timber as it comes off the rack and immediately refuse any which is substandard – whether from splits, knots (too many or too large), warping or handling damage.

WEATHERED BOARDS
If selecting homegrown hardwood, avoid the boards which have been on top of the stack while it was air drying. These are usually grey, stained and sometimes

cupped, bowed or warped.
Weathering may have produced tiny fissures
throughout the surface which may run quite deep.

POCKET PLANE
Sometimes it is difficult to judge the appearance of the
timber if a sawn board is stained or dirty. Have a small
blockplane in your pocket to remove some of the
sawing ridges to expose the clean wood beneath. Check
with the yard staff first that they don't mind, and
remove only a few discreet shavings.

KEEPING TABS ON STOCKS
If you have a particular need for a good quantity of fine
quality stuff, ask when the next load is coming in for
sale and try to be first in the queue!

ROOFRACK
Some yards might deliver boards, but can you wait that
long? Buy a pair of heavy ladder racks for the roof of
your car. Treat yourself to a new hank of rope. Keep a
yellow duster on a piece of string to tie to the end of
your load if it overhangs the car by more than a couple
of feet.

The Cutting List

CALCULATION
List all your components according to the thickness of
the sawn timber required. Add up their widths and
lengths in a very approximate manner, rounding the
figures up at every stage. A hypothetical plank of 1"
timber, 12" wide and 12' long represents one cubic foot.
If it's three-quarters that width (or length) it's ¾cu'.

LENGTH OR WIDTH?
Have in mind the components of your project when
selecting boards. Calculate the optimum lengths of the
boards, allowing wastage of say 150mm (6") at either

end for splits.

WASTAGE

Don't underestimate the amount of wastage involved in converting a rough sawn board into useful components. All in all you can allow an extra 25% to 60% for wastage.

STANDARD SIZES

Trees are sawn into a variety of imperial thicknesses. They are usually sawn well oversize because seasoning will shrink the timber across the grain. The commonest thicknesses are 1", 1½" and 2" which will plane down to 19mm-21mm (¾"-13/16") – maybe even 22mm (⅞") if it is generously sawn. Sometimes ¾" sawn is available which is useful for planing down to 16mm (⅝") or 13mm (½") for drawer components or small articles. 3" and 4" boards are also available in some timbers, especially those suitable for turning like sycamore and lime. Do not expect these thicker boards to be as thoroughly dry as the thinner ones. A 4" lump of oak will take many years to season.

CUBIC FOOTAGE

Hardwoods are calculated and priced in cubic feet. Some yards will mark their boards in square footage (surface area) and then multiply this by the thickness to calculate the cubic footage. Others will measure each board as it is selected. Ask about concessions for large splits, knots and milling damage like chainsaw scars – anything which reduces the usability of the wood. Negotiate this at the time of purchase.

PRICING

Timber prices vary enormously according to species, cut, and any particular characteristics of colour or grain that the wood might have. A ¾" board will be more expensive than 1" (per cubic foot) because more wastage has been involved in sawing it. A 2" board will be more expensive than 1" because it has taken longer to dry. You can usually obtain discounts for large quantities. Don't forget VAT.

DRYNESS

If you are in any doubt about the dryness of the timber you are buying, ask to borrow a moisture meter (and ask to be shown how to read it!). If the particular model requires that prongs be driven into the board, do this somewhere the holes won't spoil good wood. 12-14% moisture content is generally acceptable to a furniture maker.

Homegrown Hardwoods

HARDWOOD

Hardwood comes from deciduous trees and, as you'd expect, is usually (but not always) harder than softwood. Although correspondingly arduous to work, it rewards you by holding detail, by cutting cleanly and by finishing and wearing well. Exotic hardwoods can be so hard that hand work is almost impossible, but they will usually machine fairly obligingly. Practise on softer stuff first!

WANY-EDGED BOARDS

Homegrown English timbers (such as oak, ash, beech, sycamore, walnut) are sawn and dried as slices of a tree, complete with sap and bark and even the lichen on the bark. Often the tree has been sawn in half lengthwise so that one side of the board in the yard is straight sawn, the other, outer side remains 'wany-edged'. Examine the sap to see how many of these boards are usable.

OAK

When buying oak, look out for unusual colour and markings. The most dramatic cut is quarter sawn which shows the silver flashes of the medullary ray. It is also the most stable, being less likely to warp as it dries.

ASH

Take care when selecting ash that the colour will match in the finished project. Ash often has a deeper tan and brown heartwood. This is called olive ash because of its similarity with olivewood and can be very attractive. Equally, plain white ash has a strong appeal; it is light, strong and easily worked.

BEECH

Use beech more for its structural strength rather than for any visual appeal. Although dull in grain pattern it takes a stain well and is correspondingly cheap! It holds nails and tacks close to the edge and is therefore most often used for upholstered chair frames. Fairly stable when dry but can build up tensions while it is still seasoning.

WALNUT

Choose walnut for your finest work. One of the prize English cabinet timbers (with its plainer, milder American cousin), it is a streaked rich chocolate brown, soft and easy to work, producing a high shine with ease. Correspondingly expensive!

YEW

Probably the most magnificent English timber. Yew has a hard pale sapwood and an even harder heartwood which begins bright yellow/orange and mellows to a toffee brown. It might be expensive on all counts but is very rewarding and superb for most small work including turning.

SYCAMORE

More often considered as a garden weed but it does produce a lovely creamy white timber which turns very well. Rather tough for cabinetwork but can give stunning results, especially if contrasted with darker timbers. Keep an eye out for the highly prized 'ripple' sycamore.

Imported Hardwoods

STRAIGHT-EDGED BOARDS
Imported timber will have had the bark and most of the sap sawn away and discarded in the country of origin. This saves on shipping costs as the straight-edged boards can be stacked and bound in blocks. Most imported timber is plainer and less interesting than English but involves far less wastage and, especially on large jobs, can be considerably more economical. You can be fairly sure of consistent quality without inspection.

AMERICAN OAK
Usually straight grained and of a slightly more silvery colour than English. Favoured for large jobs like kitchens, shop fittings or libraries.

AMERICAN CHERRY
A popular but expensive pinkish-brown timber. It machines well, holds detail and finishes easily. Suitable for fine cabinetwork but not available in wide boards.

BRAZILIAN MAHOGANY
Brazilian mahogany is soft and plain in everything but colour. Particularly good for carving as it holds detail. Used extensively for window frames and front doors, but turns grey when exposed to the weather.

Softwood

Softwood is the timber produced by evergreen narrow-leaved coniferous trees. Growth is fast and all year round, resulting in a timber with wide annular rings which is relatively soft, although some softwoods are harder than some hardwoods – the hardwood-softwood classification is a generalisation. Softwoods tend to be resinous and do not take stain or polish well. They do not hold detail as the wood is spongy and liable to split.

Do not expect softwood to be properly dried and allow for considerable shrinkage.

SOFTWOOD GRADING
Joinery quality softwood is rated according to defects and size of knots. Descriptions of grades vary according to the country of origin. Common grades (in descending order of merit) are 1st, 4th & 5th. No-one seems to know where 2nd and 3rds have gone. More confusing is that 'unsorted' isn't the stuff they couldn't be bothered with, but the best! Don't pretend to know it all – ask.

PAR
PAR stands for 'planed all round', otherwise known as 'prepared'. This is better quality softwood than sawn constructional timber. Check its condition. It should be straight, clean and free of handling damage. Minor end splits are acceptable. The finest joinery softwood is sold in sawn boards for preparation in the workshop.

MOULDINGS
Using a router table or a spindle moulder (or even a moulding plane) you can produce many different profile mouldings. These decorative touches can make or break the look of a piece of furniture. Manufactured mouldings (pine or ramin) are available in racks from superstores and builders' merchants. (*Fig. 1*)

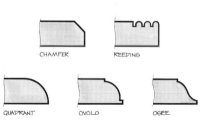

CHAMFER   REEDING

QUADRANT   OVOLO   OGEE

FIG. 1

NATURAL DURABILITY
Consider naturally weather-resistant timbers for outdoor work. Yew will stand up to the elements well, as will oak which needs no added protection to assist it. Teak is a very dense and oily timber which resists most treatment including chemical spillage and persistent sea-water. Iroko is a cheaper softer substitute with

similar properties.

The Choice Of Cuts

THROUGH AND THROUGH

The simplest and cheapest way to saw up a log is to saw a flat on one face then, resting the log on that face, take off slice after slice of wood like a grocer cutting ham. This produces boards cut through the centre of the log and through the length of the log which are known as "sawn through and through". They contain both crown-cut boards and quarter-sawn boards. The latter pass through the very centre of the tree: the former don't. (*Fig. 2*)

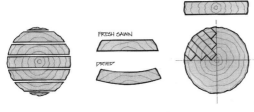

FIG. 2

FRESH SAWN

DRIED

CUTS/CROWN

Avoid crown-cut boards because they are more likely to cup as they dry. Crown-cut softwood exhibits the growth rings in wide bands as they have been cut through on the slant. The same tree quarter-sawn would show narrow bands, close together.

CUTS/QUARTER

Quarter-sawn timber is superior timber because it is less likely to cup as it dries. It does lose more overall width than crown-cut as it shrinks. The appearance of the grain is very different to crown-cut, with finer, straighter markings.

DEEP SAWING

When a thick board is sawn into two thinner boards, it is said to be deep-sawn. To 'deep' a dry board with a circular saw involves a lot of wastage, so the operation is carried out on a 're-saw' which is a very large bandsaw with a wide but thin blade. Very thin boards can be produced in this way but they should be stored flat separated by battens to permit air circulation (and further drying) and weighted to restrict warping and general distortion.

MEDULLARY RAYS
Look out for these markings in some quarter-sawn timber. They are due to a food storage system in some hardwood trees. When the log is cut across, they can be seen to radiate out from the centre like spokes in a bicycle wheel.

SAP
Take account of the sap when selecting boards. Sap is the wood that has most recently been produced by the tree. It is lighter in weight (and often in colour) than the relatively inert heartwood. In some species it is apparent as a paler band next to the bark, 10-50mm (½-2") wide, but in others is indiscernible.

HEART
Heartwood is the core timber beneath the sap layer. It provides the structural strength of the tree. It is harder, more stable and often darker than sapwood. Some ash trees have a heartwood much darker brown and with a grain pattern quite unlike the newer wood. Take care when selecting timber such as this that the colouring will be evenly displayed on the finished article.

GRAINS
Look at the grain direction on the edges of the boards you are considering buying. Ideally, a straight grained board will show grain direction parallel to, or running at, a very gentle angle to the faces. These boards will be strong and easy to plane. Occasionally you will see a very steep grain direction on the edge of a board, crossing quickly from one face to another. This will not plane easily and will be weak because of 'short grain'. If the grain direction waves up and then down along the

side of the board, they will be virtually impossible to plane. If however, these waves are about as far apart as peas in a pod, you're looking at rippled timber which is devilish to plane (better to sand it) but quite spectacular when polished.

COLOUR
If you want to know the colour of an unfinished piece of timber, wet it, either with water or with methylated spirit.

BURR
Use burred timber for decorative effect rather than for structural components. It is formed by the numerous whiskery growths on the swollen bases of old trees, notably oak, walnut, ash and elm. Try to buy two consecutive boards so that an area of burr can be 'bookmatched' with its mirror image on the next plank.

Possible Defects

SHRINKAGE
This is not a defect but it can cause them. All timber shrinks across the grain as it loses moisture. A board can lose as much as 10% of its width in the change from living tree to seasoned timber. It is not, however, all one way traffic. The driest wood can pick up moisture from a damp atmosphere (even a humid day) and expand. The whole business of solid timber construction is orientated around this fact. Never think that by gluing or screwing timber down you will prevent this movement. The wood will simply crack.

CUPPING AND BOWING
Look at the ends of the boards in the yard. All but quarter-sawn stuff is likely to be slightly bent. If it is too distorted, wide components will not be possible without a lot of planing.

WARPING

It is rare to find a badly warped board in a good yard, but always look along the board to check. Warping is general wavy distortion, as if the board is trying to set sail. It might occur if the board has uneven stresses caused by large knots, or if it has lain at the top of a pile while air-drying.

CURVED BOARDS

Just as a tree trunk might curve over, so some boards will be banana-shaped. Do not dismiss these out of hand. Often they would involve too much wastage to be a good buy but occasionally, if your project involves long angled or curved components, these boards might be exactly what you are looking for.

KILNING DEFECTS

Look closely at the surface of the sawn board. If you see patterns of small gaps where the fibres have separated, you may have some badly kilned stock. Similarly on end grain watch for tiny fissures running through the board.

KNOTS

The best timber will be taken from the straight trunk of the tree before it branches out and may well involve no knots at all. The odd small branch might leave a knot which appears through the boards. Some tree species (like yew) are naturally bushier and therefore knottier. Knots can look wonderful but are a pain to the woodworker. The grain direction is interrupted, making good planing all but impossible. Knots are of much harder wood than their surroundings and will dull blades and be scorched by a power saw. They are structurally unreliable.

SHAKES

Shakes are splits which occur in timber sometimes as it is felled and almost always as it dries. Expect to see

splits down the very centre of a wide board and think of
the board rather as two smaller boards waiting to be
separated.

STAINS
Hardwood boards in a yard can look most unappealing
with a variety of watermarks and surface staining.
Almost all of this is only skin deep. Look closely for grey
flecking which might signify a fungal infection which
runs much deeper. Be wary of sycamore if it looks at all
discoloured: it may be that the timber has been poorly
seasoned and has lost the bright whiteness, for which it
is famed, forever.

QUALITY
The combination of cut, straightness, dryness and
colour amounts to the overall quality of the stock.
Expect to pay different prices in different yards because
their products and their marketing will vary. Always
examine hardwood before you buy it.

Timber Preparation

MACHINING
When the rough timber has been converted into neat
square-edged planed components, well over half the
work has been done. Nothing beats good heavy
machines for preparation. If you don't have your own,
chat up someone who does.

MACHINING SERVICES
Many yards offer a machining service. Specify as clearly
as you can what it is that you want them to do. If a long
board can be cross-cut before being planed, there will
be less planing, resulting in thicker timber than if the
whole board is planed in one. If only one side of the
board is to be seen (as in a table-top) specify that you
want one good and one perfect surface. The side that is
merely good might still show some sawmarks. Ask what

they will charge. Ask if you can be there to watch progress.

MARKING OUT
If several boards are involved in a project, the easiest way to appreciate what you've got is to stand them outside your workshop on end. With your cutting list, a tape measure and a piece of chalk, you can make the first strokes towards ensuring that the best timber is used for the most visible components, that the colour and grain patterns will balance on the finished piece, and that as little wastage as possible is entailed.

DIMENSIONING
Cross-cut boards into manageable lengths, allowing an inch or so on every length as a safety margin. Plane one edge then use it as a guide to saw the overall width (plus a bit).

PLANING
Plane one face then one edge square to it. Thickness the board from the first face and then saw and plane the final width from the first edge.

Storage

STORING SHORT TERM
Thin stuff such as panels should be stored under weighted battens directly after planing, unless it is to be used immediately.

STORING LONG TERM
Keep surplus boards in a dry area with some ventilation. Raise the bottom board off the floor with a couple of stout pieces of softwood and interleave subsequent layers of timber with thin clean battens.

ACCLIMATIZATION
The best procedure is to roughly prepare timber for a

project some months before it is used. Store it in an atmosphere similar to that which the finished project will enjoy (this usually means 'central heating').

Timber Conversion

SAWING YOUR OWN
You will be offered trees and branches from time to time. Unless you are a fully equipped woodsman with chain mill and landrover, think twice.

AIR-DRIED/KILNED
Timber must be dried of its sap before it is usable. Logs will not dry in the round but must be sawn into boards and stacked so that the air can circulate freely. Most timber benefits from gentle drying in the open air (protected from rain and sun) before it is finished off in a kiln where the temperature and the humidity are monitored. Timber which has only been air dried may be satisfactory if it has been subject to weeks of dry summer weather.

PLANKING
Be at the sawing, either to ensure you get the thicknesses and the cuts you want or as a silent observer. Few things are as exciting as opening a tree.

BUYING GREEN
You can make considerable savings by buying fresh sawn 'green' timber and seasoning it yourself. Remember though that there will be a failure rate which even the professionals cannot predict.

THINK AHEAD
The surest way of laying hands on good timber is to already have it! If you have the space (and the cash) start a stockpile. Keep it dry and it will accrue value like a cellar of wine – but will last considerably longer.

TOOLS & TECHNIQUES

Adhesives

Mixing epoxy resin adhesives can be a messy and sticky job. Cut one side from a strong plastic bag and open it. Use the opposite corner for mixing the adhesive and hardener. A lolly stick is useful. Snip off the corner. Extrude and spread the mixture. No claggy cleaning up to do, just throw the lot into the dustbin! (*Fig. 1*)

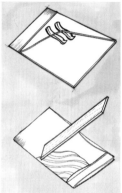

FIG. 1

Shower gel bottles make very efficient dispensers for PVA glue simply because the glue is always at the nozzle end. Train your family to prefer the kind with a spigot in the cap. This keeps the nozzle clear of hardened glue. Other dispensers such as squeezy washing up liquid bottles are fine, but when only partly filled, the glue can take a long time to flow from the bottom to the nozzle. (*Fig. 2*)

Some spray-can nozzles clog-up with maddening rapidity. Perhaps spray-glue cans are the worst. Keep spare nozzles in a strong solvent such as Evostik Cleaner in a well-sealed screw-top container. Use a bicycle pump to blow the gunge from inside the nozzle.

Before using hot-melt adhesives, do as the old woodworkers did when using hot Scotch Glue. Warm the surfaces to be glued.

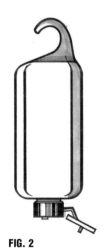

FIG. 2

Hot-melt adhesives are good for the otherwise difficult job of gluing acrylic resin plastics to wood.

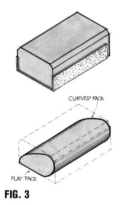

FIG. 3

Contact adhesive should be "touch-dry" before bringing them together. Test with a knuckle. If it comes away dry, then the glue is ready.

Adhesives will not stick to dusty surfaces. Scrub the edges of chipboard with a brass brush before applying adhesive or iron-on edge-banding.

Superglues (Cyanoacrylate adhesives) are good for re-gluing small splits, but do not use an accelerator if the parts are still "hinged" together. The glue sets before the parts can make intimate contact.

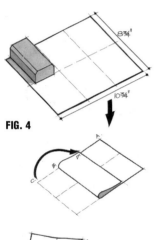

FIG. 4

FIG. 5

To convert standard cork sanding blocks to specially shaped blocks for curved work, use a rasp, then coarse sandpaper. (*Fig. 3*)

Sandpaper is expensive. Don't waste money by tearing sheets any old how. The cork sanding blocks are designed to fit one-sixth of a sheet. (*Fig. 4*)

For fine sanding with the paper held directly by the fingers, a one-sixth part of a full sheet is often re-folded into four. Tear half-way along one fold and fold it the way we illustrate. This prevents two abrasive surfaces spoiling each other by rubbing together. (*Fig. 5*)

For some tasks, a narrow, abrasive strip can be best. Make a holder for a strip taken from half of a one-sixth sized piece of sandpaper. The plastic edging strip is sold in DIY stores (by Trent Plastics) for 5/8" thick man-made boards. You can buy thin cork sheet from model-maker's suppliers. (*Fig. 6, following page*)

Use a decorator's seaming roller for spreading adhesive over a wide surface.

Bench

For quality cabinet-making, a flat bench top is important. When ripping with wood held in the vice, use an offcut to prevent damage from the saw. (*Fig. 7*)

Hardened glue spots on a bench top can wreak havoc with the surface of workpieces. Remove them as soon as they occur.

Keep the bench top clear of chippings. If they get between the top and a workpiece, when mortising, for example, they can bruise the surface of the job.

Make a cam-controlled bench stop for easy adjustment of the planing stop. Set out the radii at 1.143m (45") intervals and join the marks with a smooth curve. (*Fig. 8*)

How many times have you had to ferret amongst the shavings under your bench to find something that has fallen and rolled underneath? Fit footboards and save your knees and temper. (*Fig. 9*)

To increase the stability of your bench, add a strong shelf for heavy things. If the grain of the wood runs from front to back, it is less likely to wear as items are dragged forwards for lifting.

Primitive though it looks, the traditional bench hook (or sawing board) is not always the easiest device to handle, especially if roughly made. It will be unsteady if the main board is made from solid timber that has warped, so use plywood instead. Fit

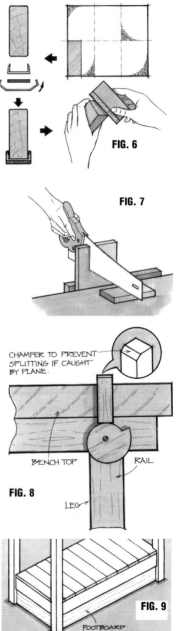

FIG. 6

FIG. 7

CHAMFER TO PREVENT SPLITTING IF CAUGHT BY PLANE.

BENCH TOP   RAIL

FIG. 8

LEG

FIG. 9

FOOTBOARD

FIG. 10

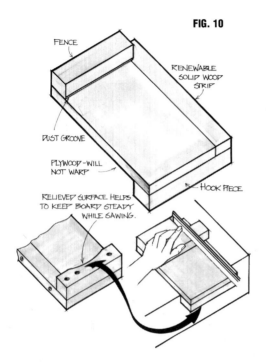

FENCE

RENEWABLE SOLID WOOD STRIP

DUST GROOVE

PLYWOOD - WILL NOT WARP

RELIEVED SURFACE HELPS TO KEEP BOARD STEADY WHILE SAWING.

HOOK PIECE

replaceable solid wood strips to take the saw overrun. If there is dust between the fence and the workpiece, the job cannot be held securely in the nook, so plane a dust groove as shown on the drawing. Movement can be prevented by gripping the hook in the vice, but this fiddly solution can hinder production. To reduce the chance of rocking against any unevenness in the front edge of the bench top, relieve the face of the hook-batten, as illustrated. The snag with this de-luxe version is that it is not possible to use both sides. (*Fig. 10*)

FIG. 11

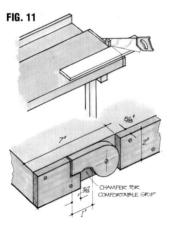

5/8"

7"

2"

3/8"

CHAMFER FOR COMFORTABLE GRIP

1"

Add a pivoted sawing stop to the end of your bench for a quick way of supporting material while sawing. (*Fig. 11*)

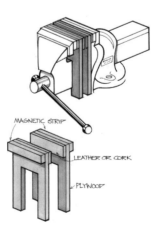

MAGNETIC STRIP

LEATHER OR CORK

PLYWOOD

FIG. 12

Sometimes an engineer's vice is best for holding some jobs. Make cork or leather-faced chops from plywood. The magnets hold them in place and can be re-cycled from an old fridge or freezer door seal. When using a contact adhesive to fix them, make sure that the most magnetic face of the rubber magnets will contact the metal of the vice. (*Fig. 12, previous page*)

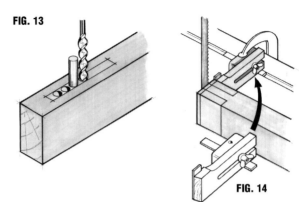

FIG. 13

FIG. 14

Joint making

Larger sizes of mortise are best made by drilling out the waste and then trimming the sides and ends. To prevent the drill drifting into an adjacent hole, temporarily plug it with a piece of dowel. (*Fig. 13*)

It is often difficult to get a bandsaw to saw parallel to the fence. Sometimes the fence can be adjusted to compensate, but the re-adjustment can be inconsistent and time-consuming. Try this "single-point" or "edge-type" fence. The sizes are suitable for a small bandsaw, but they can easily be adapted to suit your own machine. The brass strip is optional, but being detachable, it can be replaced with a longer one for deep-cutting, wider material. (*Fig. 14*)

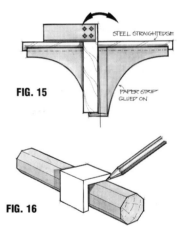

FIG. 15

STEEL STRAIGHTEDGE

PAPER STRIP GLUED ON

FIG. 16

MARKING OUT

From time to time, ensure successful work by testing your try squares, especially the larger ones. This device uses a steel straightedge for extra accuracy. A line drawn, say with the stock of the square to the left, should exactly match one drawn with the stock flipped over to the right. (*Fig. 15, previous page*)

FIG. 17

FIG. 18

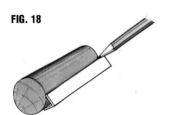

A try square will not reliably fit on hexagonal/octagonal legs and suchlike. Instead, use a shop-made angle-piece for marking out joints. (*Fig. 16, previous page*)

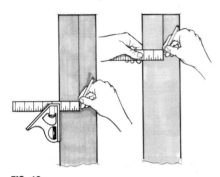

Use that broken steel tape measure you could not throw away. Use it for marking shoulders round cylindrical work. (*Fig. 17, previous page*)

Use a piece of "bright-drawn mild steel angle" for marking along the length of cylindrical work. (*Fig. 18*)

Two ways of gauging a parallel pencil line some distance from an edge. If there is a risk of splinters from unplaned wood, use the combination square.(*Fig. 19*)

FIG. 19

Only use a pencil with a shop-made gauge for marking chamfers. You could combine several sizes on one block, but since there is a risk of mistakes, it might be

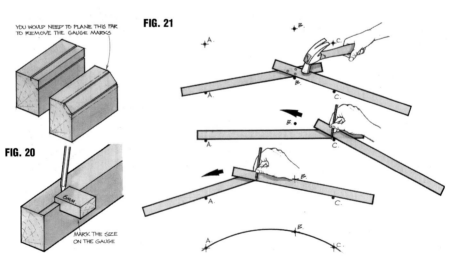

YOU WOULD NEED TO PLANE THIS FAR TO REMOVE THE GAUGE MARKS

FIG. 21

FIG. 20

MARK THE SIZE ON THE GAUGE

FIG. 22

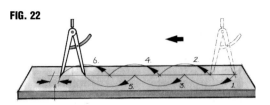

better to make several, one for each of your preferred sizes. The drawing shows what happens if a gauge is used. (*Fig. 20, previous page*)

How to draw a circular arc when there is nowhere to locate a centre. It is based on the converse of the geometrical theorem that "angles at the circumference of a circle, standing on the same chord, are equal". (*Fig. 21, previous page*)

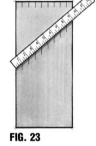

FIG. 23

To divide a length into an equal number of parts, say six, use dividers by trial and error. First guess a setting. Lightly step out the distance six times. Estimate one sixth of the error, add or subtract this to/from the original setting and try again. Avoid making too many deep divider marks. When you have got it right, locate the correct divider marks with a pencil. (*Fig. 22*)

FIG. 24

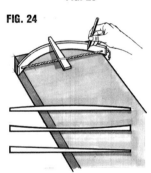

How to use a ruler to divide a width into an equal number of parts, nine in this example. (*Fig. 23*)

This is an old dodge for marking non-circular curves, but did you know that the shape can be subtly tuned by using tapered splines? (*Fig. 24*)

FIG. 25

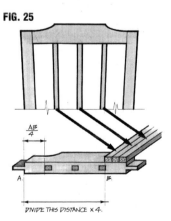

How to ensure equal spaces between rails, for example in a chair back. (*Fig. 25*)

FIG. 26

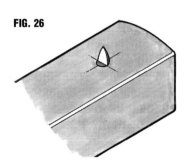

Conical gauge points tend to

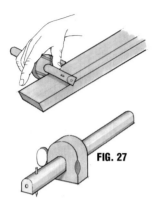

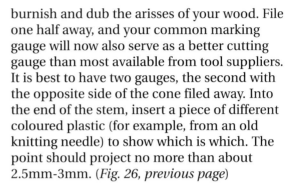

FIG. 27

burnish and dub the arises of your wood. File one half away, and your common marking gauge will now also serve as a better cutting gauge than most available from tool suppliers. It is best to have two gauges, the second with the opposite side of the cone filed away. Into the end of the stem, insert a piece of different coloured plastic (for example, from an old knitting needle) to show which is which. The point should project no more than about 2.5mm-3mm. (*Fig. 26, previous page*)

FIG. 28

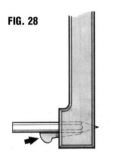

When using the marking gauge, the thumb should press on the stem as near to the point as possible. File a notch in the corner of the stock to make a more comfortable grip. (*Fig. 27*)

Make this extra stem to fit a pencil to your marking gauge. Useful for many jobs, including marking chamfers. (*Fig. 28*)

FIG. 29

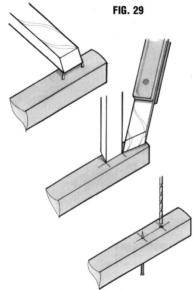

The screw in the stock of a modern mortise gauge usually tightens on to the brass slide bearing the moveable point (and if tightened too hard, can distort it). First set the distance between the points to the size of the chisel, but do not use the traditional tap on one or other of the ends to adjust the stock.

There is a risk of accidentally changing the point setting as well, especially if the brass slide has worn loose. The best gauges have the moving-point adjustment screw running inside the stock, but they are no longer made, although sometimes still available from dealers in antique tools.

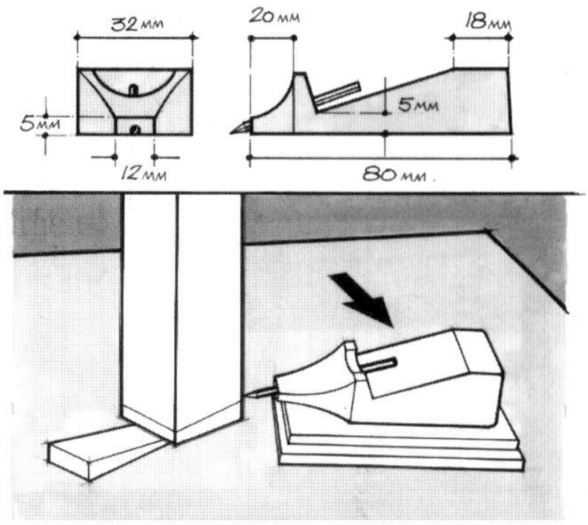

FIG. 30

Most workers own only one mortise chisel of each size. Since modern gauges may not be as good as they look and can be expensive, why not make a number of ordinary marking gauge stems with fixed points to match your own chisels? (*Fig. 29, previous page*)

The chisel should just fit between the very tips of the points. Accurately mark the centres for the points and start the drill from the exit side. Masonry nails 2.5mm in diameter make good points, but re-grind and polish the points to a smooth conical shape. The grinding marks should run lengthwise from the point. Arrange this by grinding the head away. Fit the nail into a hand-drill chuck or pin-vice and rotate the nail against a grinding wheel. It may be better not to be tempted to fit several different sets of points on each face of one stem since you run the risk of making mistakes and a likelihood of pricking or scratching yourself into the bargain.

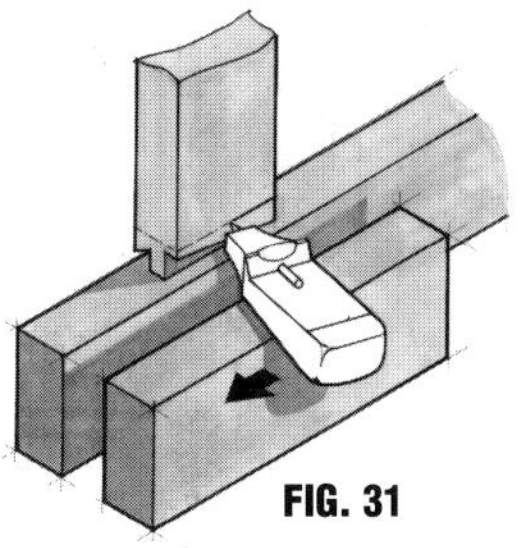

FIG. 31

Make this little mouse (*Fig. 30*) which will be useful for when you are trimming table legs to length. Set the job on a flat and level surface. Use wedges under the ends of the legs to make sure you get the top really level. Use bits of plastic sheet or man-made board to pack the mouse to reach just above the widest gap between the leg and the surface. The point will cut best if it is "trailed" to make an acute angle with the leg's surface. See also the hint about the shape of marking gauge points on the previous page.
Another use for a mouse, this time for re-marking

FIG. 32

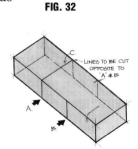

FIG. 33

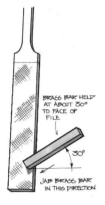

BRASS BAR HELD AT ABOUT 30° TO FACE OF FILE

30°

JAB BRASS BAR IN THIS DIRECTION

the shoulder of a badly cut tenon. When rectifying errors, it is always best to cut back to a fresh, accurately-marked cut line. Rest the mouse on an accurately-planed piece of wood the same width as the stile. (*Fig. 31, previous page*)

If, for example, you are transferring marks from say, the face edge of a rail to the opposite edge, as when marking out a through-mortise, to cut right across as at "C" is only to give yourself extra work. The line will have to be removed at the cleaning-up stage. Simply making a small nick on the opposite corner will serve just as well. (*Fig. 32, previous page*)

Files

Files can easily become blocked with metal that jams between the teeth, especially when working with aluminium. Rubbing the file with chalk can sometimes be a preventative, and a special wire brush made from "file card" helps to clean a pinned file. For more obstinate particles, jabbing along the lines of the furrows between the teeth with the end of a piece of brass bar, tube or rod should do the trick. The brass should measure about 10mm (⅜") across. If this fails, you'll have to pick out particles one-by-one with a sharp steel point such as a scriber. (*Fig. 33*)

The teeth at the end of a rasp or dreadnought file can be quite sharp. Bind the end with insulation tape to cover the place where you grip it between your finger and thumb. It pays to get into the habit of always cleaning a file or rasp before putting it away, especially after use on "green" wood. If left in contact with metal for a while some woods can corrode the teeth.

Oily files will not cut metals properly. Prevention is better than cure, but clean contaminated files with paraffin or a solvent such as Evostik Cleaner.

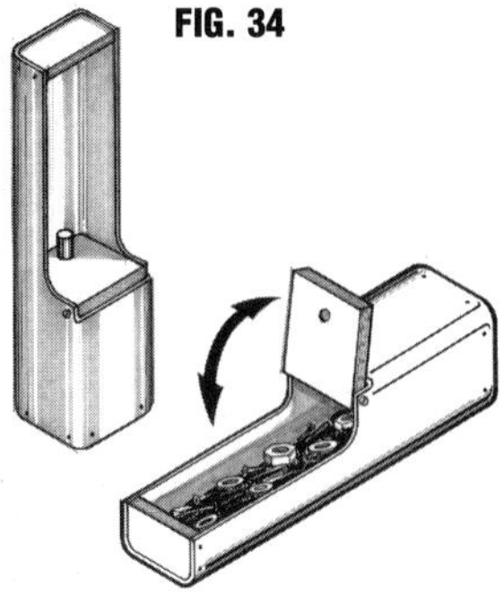

FIG. 34

Housekeeping

Use 50mm (2") square rainwater fall pipe to make this combined storage and sorting device for your bits and bobs. No more scrabbling on the floor for the parts that got away! (*Fig. 34*)

Tools that become magnetised can be a nuisance when they pick up steel filings. They can be demagnetised by stroking them over the metal laminations of an energised mains transformer or a record player motor with the rotor removed. If you make a gadget for this purpose, ensure that all electrical connections are safe and the metal is earthed.

Slender offcuts and dowels can be conveniently stored in various lengths of 50mm (2") square rainwater fall pipe. Stick them together with Clear Bostik or similar adhesive.

Make a rule – never have more than (say) ten tools on the bench top at a time.

Make another rule. Immediately replace caps and lids on containers to prevent spills, or prevent harmful fumes invading the workshop.

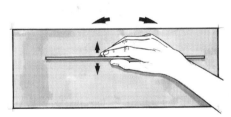

FIG. 35

Do not use linseed oil as an oilstone lubricant, or to prevent metal rusting. It will form a gummy skin.

Planing

Test for nicks in a ruler's edge from time to time. They can prevent the rule from giving a true reading when testing a surface.

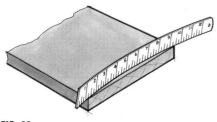

FIG. 36

When testing a surface with a rule, one sometimes has to hold work up to the light to see the amount of error, but time and energy can be saved by testing the feel of a steel rule. The ends will be held by a hollow surface so the rule can be flexed. The rule will swivel on a convex surface. (*Fig. 35, previous page*)

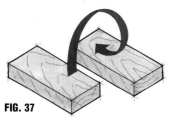

FIG. 37

There is a good chance that your steel rule is slightly bowed. Unless its face is held at right-angles to the surface under test, a false convex or concave reading may result. The thicker rules fitted to good quality combination squares are less likely to have this defect, but beware of very cheap tools of this kind. The edges might not be accurate enough. (*Fig. 36*)

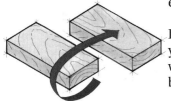

If, when planing both sides of a workpiece, you half-somersault the wood end-to-end when turning it over, the grain direction will be maintained. (*Fig. 37*)

To protect the sole and cutting iron of your planes, inspect the wood for grit before starting work. The ends of boards are particularly likely to pick up grit from the floor or the merchant's yard.

Plane very small pieces by pushing them over a plane mounted upside down in the vice. Be careful not to break the sides of cast-iron planes by severe over-tightening.

When a plane is used on a shooting board, use a straight-edged blade. The shooting board fixes the angle of the edge, so a cambered edge to the blade is unnecessary and may actually throw the edge angle out-of-square.

Screwing And Nailing

FIG. 38

Wood screws are easier to fit (and remove) if lubricated with a spot of tallow or lard. Make a "dab-pot" to hold the fat. The handle on the lid makes it easier to operate with one hand. (*Fig. 38*)

When entering a screw into an existing thread, turn the screw backwards until it can be felt to click slightly forwards. When this happens, the leading edge of the male thread has just passed the start of the matching thread. It is then safe to turn forwards without the risk of cross-threading.

The point of a sharp nail or panel pin tends to slip between the wood fibres, forcing them apart and so splitting the wood, especially near the end of a board. Flatten the end of a nail to make it cut and crush the fibres instead. Sometimes it is best to drill a pilot hole.

FIG. 39

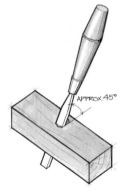

If you need to grip the threaded part of a bolt in a metalworker's vice, wrap thick copper wire round the threads so that the vice grips on the wire instead of crushing the threads. Offcuts of electrician's cable are a useful source of copper wire if you can get hold of them.

Screwing directly into the end-grain of wood is unreliable. Drill holes for plastic masonry plugs and screw into them.

Keep the hammer face clean. Dirty hammer faces are a common cause of bent nails.

Tools

A temporary Old Woman's Tooth router can be made by driving a narrow chisel (preferably a bevelled-edge firmer chisel) into a close-fitting hole in a block of hardwood. Drill the hole at about 45 degrees to the base. Although it will be a bit top-heavy when not in use, and may take a time to set the cutter to the right depth, it can serve quite well for such tasks as the final levelling of the bottom of a housing joint. (*Fig 39, previous page*)

FIG. 40

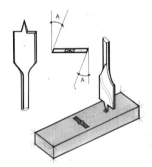

A chisel is traditionally used for sharpening pencils, but the harder grades of pencil will soon dull the edge. The graphite left on the back face can transfer dirty marks to a job. Therefore keep an old chisel for sharpening pencils.

FIG. 41

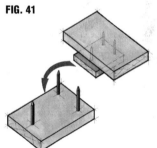

Chisels lend themselves to uses for odd-jobs such as scraping dirt from a surface. This is hardly good for a carefully sharpened edge. Keep an old chisel for such tasks.

If you find that your chisel drifts sideways when mortising by hand, check whether the end is square to the sides.

You can make a non-standard sized drill from the next largest size of a flatbit. Grind an equal amount from each side, maintaining the angles: "A". Check the grinding by driving the bit vertically into a 4mm (5/32" approx.) hole into a piece of scrap until it makes an impression in the surface. Extract the bit, turn it for half a turn to see whether the impression exactly matches. Remove a little at a time. Keep proving the size by drilling test holes.
(*Fig. 40*)
Make several of these gadgets so that you can lacquer or paint both sides of workpieces in the same session.

Rest the job on the least important side, since the points might leave three tiny dimples in the finish. (*Fig. 41, previous page*)

For people without a metalworking lathe, here's how to make a tenon on the end of a rod, ready, for example, for threading. This is a useful dodge for making workshop gadgets and a nice test of your skill with a file. As the file runs over it, the washer should be free to rotate. Test the size by making a gauge from a piece of metal containing a hole of the diameter you want. (*Fig. 42*)

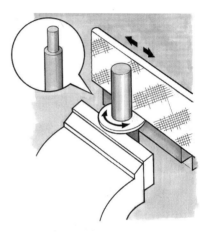

FIG. 42

SHARPENING

Introduction

Sharp tools are an absolute must for any woodworking task. Blunt tools not only make work difficult but they are difficult to control and make for inaccurate work.

Sharpening requires skill, good technique and above all practice to get consistent results. I must stress that there are as many ways of sharpening as there are people enjoying woodwork and the methods listed below are those which have served me well for many years. If you wish to adapt them to your ways then that's fine, but above all consistency is the key to success.

Safety

To ensure continued enjoyment from your woodwork it is essential that any sharpening functions are carried out in a safe manner. Always wear goggles or a face mask when using any powered grinder and always read the instruction manual carefully before operating a new or unfamiliar machine.

Grinding Wheels

There are many types of grinding wheel and for edge tools I prefer those that run in a water-bath such as the Tormek. These produce good results if used with a certain amount of care and have the advantage that it is possible to see clearly what is happening.

If you are using the standard type of offhand grinder, in other words the pedestal type, then it is essential that a water-bath into which it is possible to frequently quench the tool being ground is close at hand. Dip the tool often to prevent overheating.

Any tool rest should be placed as close as possible to the revolving wheel. This will support the tool being sharpened and will also prevent small items such as a twist drill from becoming trapped between the wheel and tool holder. I would consider a gap of an eighth of an inch too large.

A high speed offhand grinder is not really suitable for the grinding of hand tool cutters; things happen much too fast and it is all too easy to burn the cutting edge. If you are buying a grinder for the first time, then I would strongly recommend something like the Tormek that runs in water and is wide enough for the full width of the cutting edge.

Any grinding wheel of whatever type will need to be dressed down from time to time. This is the process of removing the top layer from the stone to expose new grit. Dressing down also removes irregularities from the wheel and restores the wheel to a flat and true surface. A wheel is dressed in one of two ways, either using a special tool called a star dresser or by using a devil stone. These are available from reputable tool suppliers and I strongly recommend that the instructions which come with either one are followed to the letter to avoid any possible injury from the carborundum grit that is removed.

Saws

When sharpening saws, particularly for the less experienced, practise on the largest saw that you have. This may seem contrary to expectations but larger teeth make it easier to see what you are doing and mistakes are easier to spot on the larger sizes. When you have fully mastered the techniques then that is the time to move onto the smaller saws.

Before a saw can be sharpened it usually needs to be set. This is the method of bending alternate teeth in opposite directions to give adequate clearance to the saw cut and to prevent binding. (*Fig. 1*)

Saws are set with a pair of setting pliers that are specifically designed for the purpose. No other tools should be used because this is one of those times when an improvised solution just will not work.

Around the anvil of the setting pliers are numbers and these refer to the number of teeth per inch of blade. Therefore, a rip saw with three teeth per inch should be set with the number three on the setting pliers uppermost.

When setting a saw you may find it useful to be in the sitting position. Work from the handle down towards the end, bending each alternate tooth, and tuck the saw handle under your arm as you work for greater control. When you have done one side, turn the saw over and do the teeth you did not do on the first side.
The centre teeth on any saw tend to wear down more quickly than those at the ends, so you may wish to dress the tops of the teeth with an oilstone held flat until when sighted from either end the teeth appear perfectly flat. One word of warning here: don't overdo this, as the teeth tend to disappear at an alarming rate. Keep checking every three or four strokes.

If a saw is excessively worn then you may need to

FIG. 1

sharpen the saw twice, once after topping to restore the shape and then again after setting to deliver a sharp cutting edge.

Do not attempt to sharpen hard point saws, distinguished by a black colour to the saw tips. Any attempt to set and sharpen these could result in a tooth flying off at high speed, with serious consequences.

Saws are held in what are known as saw clamps or chops and these can be made very simply from a few bits of timber that most woodworkers will have lying around in the workshop. Alternatively, clamp the saw in two bits of wood the length of the saw blade in the bench vice. However, if you adopt this approach then it will almost certainly be necessary to sit down to sharpen your saw. What you should aim for is to sharpen the saw at elbow height, as this avoids fatigue and the teeth are close enough to the eye to avoid strain. (*Fig. 2*)

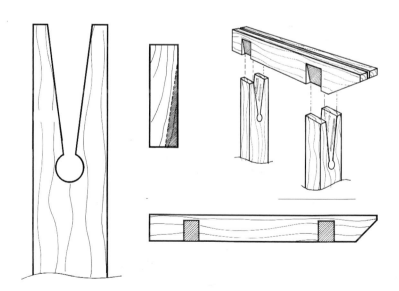

FIG. 2

37

For the best results when sharpening saws, try to get into a rhythm and do not stop or get distracted until you have finished one side. If the sharpening is stopped and then recommenced at a later time, not only will you find it hard to get back into a rhythm but it is quite possible to get the teeth uneven.

Planes

Use a honing guide for consistent results when sharpening chisels, but be extremely careful that the wheel on any such guide does not wear a ridge in the stone. Try to avoid rubbing the wheel up and down in the same place all the time and be certain to use the full width and length of the stone. Many professionals do not use a honing guide, saying that an experienced worker does not need such devices, but they do hold the blade at a more consistent angle than anybody working freehand could ever hope to achieve.

Be extremely careful not to draw the temper of any tool blade by overheating it on the grinder. Keep the blade moving and unless you have a stone which runs in water then dip the edge being ground into water at regular intervals. A blade which turns blue has almost certainly been overheated.

Grinding needs to be carried out at an angle of 25 degrees. Follow this by honing the edge to razor sharpness at an angle of 30 degrees on an oil or water stone. Rub the blade back and forth until you see a slight burr form on the back of the blade, then turn the blade over and, holding it down flat on the stone, polish off the burr that has formed.

When sharpening spokeshave blades and other small cutters, it is well worth making wooden holders. A piece of mahogany or similar hardwood approximately the width of the blade with a split in one end into which the blade fits is ideal. This way you will have something to grip and your control of the cutting operation will be that much easier and safer.

Oilstones

Many craftsmen boil their stones in petroleum jelly prior to first use as this prevents the unnecessary take-up of excessive amounts of oil and in my experience helps to keep the stone clean. However, never subject water or other natural stones to this treatment as it will ruin them.

Craftsmen and women tend to call all stones which are used for sharpening "oilstones". However, this term is not really correct, as many stones do not use oil as a cutting agent but are either intended to be used dry or with water.

When you buy any stone it should state what type of lubricant should be used when sharpening your tools. It is important to follow the manufacturer's recommendations, as an inappropriate lubricant or cutting agent will irreparably damage a new stone.

Cutting agents – be they oil, water or proprietary compound – all perform the same tasks; firstly, they provide a very thin film between the cutting edge and the stone stopping the tool from dragging unnecessarily; secondly, they hold the metal particles which are removed from the edge in suspension and prevent the stone from becoming blocked; lastly, this slurry of waste actually helps with the sharpening process by providing a secondary abrasive to the main stone and it is for this reason that the stone should not be wiped clean until the sharpening is finished.

Great care should be taken with all stones, and they should be stored away from the main woodworking area if possible to avoid getting wood dust engrained into the surface of the stone. Additionally, it is normal practice to store stones in a wooden box and most woodworkers make their own, although some of the diamond stones do come already supplied with a box. The only exception are the water stones, which need to be kept immersed in the water at all times to prevent drying out. However, this is not really a problem as the very fact that they are below the water surface prevents them from getting dirty and contaminated with dust and workshop grime.

An oilstone that has become badly clogged can be given a new lease of life by heating gently with a hot air gun. This will dislodge all the entrapped oil, grime and dirt.

Chisels

Chisels are sharpened in much the same way as plane irons, with a 25 degree grinding angle and a 30 degree sharpening angle. Be aware, however, that chisels, especially the smaller sizes, wear down rapidly on any grinder as the amount of metal that has to be removed is proportionately less.

Many new chisels when first bought are not as smooth on their backs as they ought to be. That is why I like to polish these to a high shine before I ever attempt to sharpen. If this rather laborious process is carried out, the resultant keen edge will undoubtedly pay for all the time spent.

Gouges and Carving Tools

All gouges and carving tools are sharpened little and often and, as many are on the delicate side, it pays not to put them to the grinder unless it is absolutely essential.

Gouges come in two basic types regardless of their size and these are out-cannled and in-cannled – in other words they either have the bevel on the inside or the outside. Gouges that are on the inside are obviously hard to grind and this is best achieved by not using a high speed bevelled wheel but a coarse slipstone or diamond slip.

If you buy some of the better quality gouges then these will come ready sharpened and honed to a keen edge. It is then simply a matter of following the bevel put on by the manufacturer to ensure that your tools stay sharp and bright. The secret here is little and often.

Keep the slipstones to hand when doing any carving and sharpen as soon as the tool starts to lose its edge.

Slipstones are best stored in a 50:50 mixture of oil and paraffin as this keeps them clean and also ensures that the stone is charged with lubricant ready for the next time it is required.

Drills

This is rather a loose term and tends to encompass all sorts of circular objects for boring holes with varying degrees of success. Nevertheless, as with any type of tool, to give of its best it has to be sharp. All drills can be divided into those that are sharpened with an electric grinder of some sort and those that are sharpened by using a file or small slipstone.

As a general rule, those drills which are intended for use in some form of electric drill are sharpened with recourse to the grinder, whilst those that are primarily for use by some form of hand power are sharpened with a file or slip. Of course, this can be, as forstner bits which were originally intended for use in a carpenter brace are now nearly always used in a pillar drill. One sure-fire way to check if you are unsure is to try sharpening by using a file. If that won't touch it then it is almost certain that you need to revert to the grinder. When sharpening boring bits of any description it is very important that only the barest minimum of metal is removed from the cutting edge.

Never remove any metal from the outside edge of any boring bit as this will ruin it to an extent from which there is absolutely no recovery, save throwing the offending bit away and buying another one.

MACHINERY

The Portable Router

A CUTTER SETTING DEVICE
A useful device for the quick and accurate depth setting of straight router cutters (single or two flute) for such jobs as rebating or grooving is what can best be described as the "feeler" gauge.

The gauges are pieces of hardwood (beech is excellent) about 90mm long x 20mm wide. My set consists of 6 pieces 4, 6, 8, 10, 12, and 16mm thick, they are strung together for convenience.

TO USE THE GAUGES PROCEED AS FOLLOWS:-
1) Secure the cutter in the router.
2) Plunge the router so that the cutter touches the workpiece and lock it.
3) Raise the depth-stop on the router.
4) Insert the appropriate feeler onto the depth-stop arresting screw.
5) Lower the depth-stop onto the feeler and lock it, withdraw feeler. The cutter is now set to the required depth.

FIG. 1

This device is particularly useful for those who, like me, have poor sight. (*Fig. 1*)

A ROUTING MAT
When routing, the problem of securing the workpiece to the bench frequently arises. Strips can be tacked round but they often get in the way of the routing operation. Double-sided tape is good but its application can be time consuming, particularly if a number of pieces are to be machined.

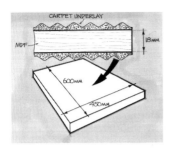

FIG. 2

A useful device for securing flat workpieces is the routing mat. These can be purchased and work very well. An alternative can be made in the workshop from carpet underlay. A piece of 18mm chipboard, MDF or ply is needed. The quality doesn't matter but it must be perfectly flat. The size is a matter of choice: mine is 450mm x 600mm. Stick underlay to both sides with impact adhesive and you will have an excellent routing mat. The workpiece will move until the weight of the router is applied, when it will be found to be quite secure. (*Fig. 2*)

CUTTER AND COLLET CARE
Many people experience the problem of cutters getting jammed in the router collet. This is frequently caused by the incorrect assembly and mounting of the collet and the collet nut. Always place the collet in the collet nut and make sure that it clicks into place, then screw the assembly onto the router. Never place the collet in the router and then screw the collet nut on, as the cutter will almost certainly jam when the collet nut is tightened.

Always insert cutters at least three-quarters of their shank length and if the shank is long and likely to butt up against the end of the motor shaft, ease it out about a millimetre. Failure to do this may set up a hammer action which could cause the cutter to work loose.

Cutters should be kept sharp, with an ordinary oilstone for high-speed steel and a diamond whetstone for TCT. Regardless of their shape, 90% of cutters have a flat inside face and it is this face that is applied to the sharpening medium. A hone after each use will ensure the maximum cutting life.

THE CENTRE FINDER
It is sometimes necessary to accurately locate the cutter

in the router at some particular point on a workpiece. To solve this problem a centre finder is the answer. (*Fig. 3*)

The finder is a piece of clear perspex about 200mm x 150mm. To make this gadget, first bolt the perspex to the base of the router, fit a small cutter in the collet, start the router and plunge through the perspex. You have now established the exact centre point. Next, scribe two lines at right angles and then enlarge the centre hole to about 50mm, all as shown in Fig 3. The finder is now ready for use. To use the centre finder, bolt it to the base of the router, line it up with the scribed lines matching the corresponding line that have been drawn on the workpiece with a suitable cutter. (*Fig. 3*)

FIG. 3

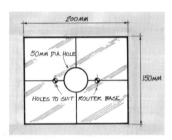

THE FENCE EXTENSION

The fence as supplied by the manufacturers of most portable routers tends to be on the short side and it can be of considerable advantage to the router user if it is extended. A close grained hardwood such as beech is ideal, about 20-25mm x 10-12mm with an overall length of about 500mm.

Ideally the fences should be slotted so that the gap can be adjusted to suit the size of the cutter. The advantages of an extended fence can be realised both at the start and at the end of any straight cut which involves the use of the side fence. A much smoother, steadier start to the cut can be made and there is no fear of "drop off" at the end of the cut if the left hand is used to steady the rear of the fence (away from the cutter). (*Fig. 4*)

FIG. 4

THE BASE EXTENSION

Many router users experience difficulty in holding the

machine steady when moulding edges using self-guiding cutters, particularly if they have a large and powerful machine.

The answer to this is a base extension. At least one manufacturer supplies this option; the majority do not.

FIG. 5

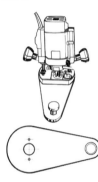

Fortunately, it is a simple device to make in the workshop. The material can be ply or MDF no more than 6mm (¼") thick (thicker will result in losing setting depth), and preferably faced with plastic laminate on the underside for smooth working. The overall dimensions are not critical and can be varied to suit the size of router. In the case of Elu routers the base extension can be attached with M5 screws into the holes for the guide bush. Most other routers have similar tapped holes. (*Fig. 5*)

THE CUTTING GAUGE

A problem that is frequently encountered when routing is break-out when rebating or moulding, and this can become quite serious when machining hardwoods that have an interlocking grain. The problem occurs at the bottom of the cut where the scraping action of the cutter causes the fibres of the material to be torn out. Of course this has been a problem with craftsmen using spindle moulders for a hundred years and was overcome by indulging in the highly dangerous (and now illegal) practice of "back cutting". This involved drawing the material backwards in the direction of the revolving cutter to obtain a clean sharp edge. This it did, but the chance of a kickback was ever present and the result could be horrific.

The simple answer is to use a cutting gauge to scribe a line at the depth of cut, and a clean, sharp edge will then result.

The gauge is also useful when cutting across grain. For

example, when panel raising, a cut line will give a clean, sharp finish to the moulding. (*Fig. 6*)

FIG. 6

The Planer/Thicknesser

SURFACE PLANER

When using the planer/thicknesser in the overhand mode the guard provided should always be used. The correct setting for the conventional "bridge" type guard is to leave a gap of not more than 9mm for the passage of the timber under or past the guard. Thus the correct setting for facing and edging material say, 150mm x 25mm, would be 34mm from the table surface to the underside of the guard whilst the end of the guard should be 34mm from the fence. This will enable the user to face and edge safely.

If short pieces are required – say 200mm (8" approx.) it's a good idea to "double up" – 400mm (16" approx.) so that they can be planed safely. However, short, wide pieces can be safely machined using a push-block. These are usually made of 18mm ply or MDF and the normal procedure is to copy a plan handle to form a comfortable grip. Care should be taken to replace the bridge guard at the completion of the cut, however, as with wide pieces a lot of the cutter block is exposed. (*Fig. 7*)

FIG. 7

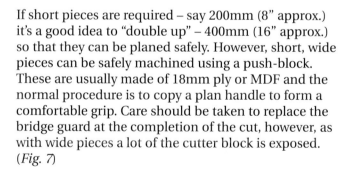

OVERHAND PLANING TIPS

The object of overhand planing is to ensure that the finished piece is straight, square and not twisted. It is a vital and fundamental woodworking operation and its importance cannot be overemphasized.

The in-feed table of the overhand function should be finely set to take a light shaving and the fence checked for square. The material should then be studied because, for example, a long piece of timber that is badly bowed will be quite unsuitable for, say, a door stile. Similarly, a very badly twisted piece would be rejected, although both timbers may well be used for short lengths.

If the material is slightly bowed in its length or hollow in its width, the bowed or hollow side should be planed. Start by removing both ends and plane until a cut can be made through the whole length of the piece. Check for straightness by eye or with a straightedge and similarly for twist, by eye or with a pair of winding strips. These are pieces of parallel hardwood about 500mm long x 70mm x 16mm (20" x 3" x ⅝" approx.) which are placed at each end of the material to show clearly the extent of any twist.

In order to achieve a straight cut the hand pressure should be kept on the out-feed table. The direction of grain can be important, but the problem can usually be overcome by taking a light cut in both directions and then planing in the direction that gives the best finish.

Once the face has been planed a face mark (usually a script type F) is made, the tail pointing to the face edge which is then planed with the face side to the fence. Check that the edge is square to the face and adjust the fence if necessary. The material is then ready for thicknessing.

Thicknessing Tips

Before commencing the thicknessing operation ensure that the thicknessing table is clean and free from any resin deposits. With a new machine it's a good idea to polish the thicknessing table until a mirror finish is obtained. This together with a little silicone will ensure the smooth passage of the material. Check also that the feed rollers are clean.

Timber, particularly hardwood, can vary in thickness and the amount taken off when overhand planing can accentuate this variation. For most thicknessers the maximum cut at one pass is 3-4mm, so when the timber thickness varies it is good practice to pass the material through the machine two or even three times. The final cut can then be made on one setting, thus ensuring that all pieces are of equal size. One safety tip is never look directly into the thicknessing area: if there is a problem look from the side.

Jointing With the Planer

The overhand function of a planer/thicknesser is ideal for producing accurate shot joints when wide panels are required made up from a number of boards. The boards are first planed and thicknessed then laid out so that the annual rings alternate, which will ensure a flat panel. Mark each joint so that it can be identified; the usual way to do this is by drawing lines across the joints, /,//,///,////, and so on, depending on the number of joints.

The planer must be sharp and finely set and the fence square. Plane each edge alternately: the first cut with the tick marks to the fence and the mating edge with the tick marks away from the fence. This will ensure that if the fence is slightly out of square the panel will be flat.

Plane the edges with a light pressure on the out-feed table.

Planing Thin Material And Multiple Planing

It is sometimes necessary to thickness a number of pieces to the same section, but putting several pieces through at the same time presents no problem if you have a modern machine fitted with anti-kickback fingers. Some old machines do not have this facility, so only single pieces should be fed. The danger is that thin pieces can be ejected, possibly injuring the operator.

Occasionally very thin material is required, thinner than the thicknesser can normally cope with. This problem can be solved by preparing a reasonably stout board and machining it to thickness. The material to be machined can then be laid on the board and the whole lot passed through the thicknesser. By this method very thin sections can be obtained. A few words of warning; not all timbers are suitable and satisfactory results will not be achieved using timbers with coarse, wild or interlocking grain. Mild, straight grained stuff is best.

Tapering And Chamfering

Although the planer/thicknesser is primarily a preparation machine, there are one or two other operations it can perform. Rebating is no longer permissible as it is considered hazardous so machines are no longer provided with a rebating facility.

Tapering to a limited extent can be done for such jobs as chair and table legs. To taper a piece the in-feed table is lowered as required, the maximum on most small planers being about 12mm. If the workpiece is too long a false fence can be clamped to the maker's fence and the back stop can be clamped to this. A back stop means that you can start the cut in the right place.

To make the cut, place the bridge guard in position and start the machine. With one end held firmly against the back stop, lower the workpiece onto the cutters and feed through steadily using a push-stock. After about halfway hold the workpiece firmly on the out-feed table with the left hand and complete the cut using the push-stock in the right hand.

Chamfering and bevelling can be done by canting the fence to the required angle. This should be done with care and always with the bridge guard in place.

PUSHSTICKS, SPIKES AND PUSHBLOCKS

Although it must be fairly obvious that a pushstick should always be accessible when spindle moulding, it is surprising how many people rely on any odd piece of timber to push the workpiece past the cutters. This is not a good idea and a properly made stick should always be on hand.

Not quite so obvious is the spike. This is a length of hardwood about 400-450mm (15¾" x 18" approx.) long (turned, if possible, for comfort), with a stout nail in one end which is ground to a point. The spike is particularly useful when it is necessary to halt the cut at any point and withdraw the workpiece, a typical example being a stopped chamfer.

FIG. 10

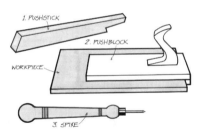

Pushblocks are very useful for machining small pieces and making end grain cuts in battens. If they are made large enough they can, for many jobs, be a substitute for a sliding table.
The blocks can be made in a variety of thicknesses to suit the job in hand. Copy a plane handle for a comfortable grip and always ensure that the block is square. (*Fig. 10*)

FRONT AND BACKSTOPS

It is frequently necessary, when working with the spindle moulder, to commence the cut other than at the end of the workpiece. This process is known as "dropping on" and can be hazardous if not carried out correctly. The danger is that the cutterblock can snatch and eject the material, damaging the workpiece and possibly injuring the operator. The danger can be overcome by fitting a backstop. This is a piece of timber that is cramped to the fence (for long jobs a fence extension may be needed) which will prevent the kickback. If a number of cuts are to be made in material that is the same length it is an advantage to also fit a front stop, which will ensure that the cut will always be the correct length. Accurate setting of the blocks can be achieved by marking the face board where the cutters enter and leave.

THE SWING STOP
A variation of the back stop that can sometimes be useful is the swing stop. A typical situation where this device could be used is when forming external rebates or moulds on window sashes. Breakout inevitably occurs when the fourth side is machined (at the end of the cut). The swing stop allows the operator to start and finish the cut in the middle, ensuring a clean finish with no corner breakout. (*Fig. 11*)

THE STARTER BLOCK
When the spindle moulder is used for shaping operations, such as shaping the segments of a semi-circular arch, there are two methods that can be employed: the ring fence and the bearing ring. The bearing ring, used in conjunction with a rebate block of similar size, is extremely useful for cleaning up shapes prior to moulding or rebating. The procedure is to make an accurate template of one segment in 9mm or 12mm and pin this to the band-sawn workpiece. The workpiece, with the template attached, is held in a suitable jig and can then be machined with the template held lightly against the bearing ring. The only possible danger of a kickback is at the commencement of the cut and this can be overcome by bolting a starter block to the table so that

FIG. 11

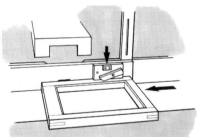

the workpiece can make the starting cut smoothly. Note that some form of guarding should always be used for this and any other spindle moulding operation. (*Fig. 12*)

FIG. 12

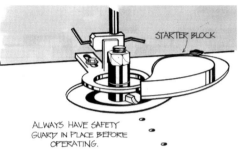

STARTER BLOCK

ALWAYS HAVE SAFETY GUARD IN PLACE BEFORE OPERATING.

A CUTTER SETTING DEVICE

Traditionally the workers that operated the spindle moulder were known as spindle hands, and these craftsmen were highly skilled. Cutter setting, to these tradesmen, was largely a matter of trial and error, but so skilled were they that there was very little error involved and they could set quickly and accurately. However, for us lesser mortals, some form of setting device can be helpful. Such a device can be simply made using a suitable piece of hardwood or ply with a couple of pieces salvaged from a broken rule. Two are needed – one for setting the height and the second for setting the depth. (*Fig. 13*)

FIG. 13

USING TOGGLE CLAMPS

One of the handiest clamps for holding workpieces is the toggle clamp. These come in a variety of sizes for both horizontal and vertical hold. The holding pressure is adjustable and when fitted with rubber heads they hold the workpiece very securely. Two examples are illustrated. Notice that the jigs are properly made, this does not mean that they are complicated, but they *are* strong. (*Fig. 14*)

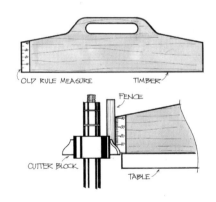

OLD RULE MEASURE   TIMBER

FENCE

CUTTER BLOCK

TABLE

CHOOSING THE RIGHT CUTTERBLOCK

For nearly sixty years the Whitehill cutterblock has

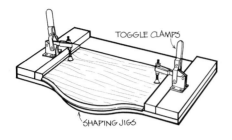

TOGGLE CLAMPS

SHAPING JIGS

FIG. 14

been the main cutterblock used by the majority of spindle moulder users. It is simple to use and very economical. Cutters can be made in the workshop and because of the way the cutter fits in the block it can be turned or angled. Many workers used just one cutter plus a balancer and it must be admitted that, with a sharp cutter and the block running at 6000rpm, a good finish can be obtained. The cutters are held in the block by clamping pressure only, so that failure to tighten the securing nut could result in the cutter being ejected with disastrous results.

Modern practice is favouring the cutterblock which has holes through the cutters through which bolts pass, eliminating the possibility of cutter ejection. In addition these blocks have limiters. These are pieces of steel the same shape as the cutter, which are fitted in front of the cutter just below the cutting circle of the block. Their purpose is twofold: to eliminate the possibility of a kickback (the workpiece being thrown back by a grabbing action) and by limiting the cutting depth, preventing serious injury if the hand should come into contact with the revolving block. These blocks are efficient and very safe but unfortunately, because two cutters and two limiters are required for each set up, they are expensive to operate.

THE BANDSAW
The bandsaw, one of the most useful machines in the workshop, also appears to be the machine that is most abused. All wood-working machinery should be kept sharp, but this applies particularly to the bandsaw. A blunt bandsaw blade is virtually useless – it will wander and even burn the workpiece. It is therefore necessary to have spare sharp blades in hand so that the change

can be made when a blade gets dull.

The next important factor to keep in mind is blade tension. Roughly when 150mm (6") of blade is exposed the blade should move about 6mm (¼") each way, the general rule being, the wider the blade the higher the tension.

A constant check should be made to ensure that the blade guides are correctly adjusted and are just clear of the blade. The wheels also should be checked periodically for wear or resin build-up. Attention to all these details will result in cleaner cutting and longer blade life.

A WEDGE CUTTING JIG

Wedges of all sizes are commonly used in all branches of woodwork. The bandsaw is the safest machine for wedge cutting, although the job can also be done on the circular saw. A piece of softwood about 100mm (4") wide x 305mm (12") thick is used, a convenient length being 300-450mm (12-16"). A wedge-shaped cut out is made in a long side the size and slope of the required wedges. A handle can be attached for convenience and safety. The material for the wedges is prepared and cut to length. The wedges can then be cut using the fence of the bandsaw. Wedges can be cut with either sharp or blunt points by simply moving the fence either way. A word of warning: when the workpiece starts to get too small, use a block to prevent the fingers getting too close to the sawblade. (*Fig. 15*)

FIG. 15

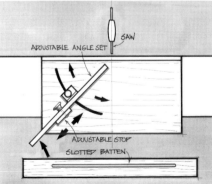

COPY SAWING WITH THE BANDSAW

Copy sawing can be performed using the bandsaw when a number of workpieces of similar size are required. Only fairly simple shapes

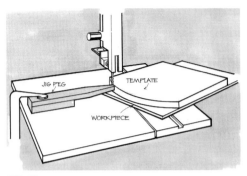

FIG. 16

should be attempted and a sharp blade of suitable width to suit the job must be used. It is first necessary to make an accurate template of the required shape in 6mm or 9mm ply. A suitable peg (preferably hardwood) is clamped to the saw table in the position shown in the illustration. The template is pinned to the timber blank and the workpiece is fed through the machine with the template in constant contact with the template. (*Fig. 16*)

TENONING WITH THE BANDSAW
The bandsaw can be used to cut accurate tenons if a few simple rules are followed. Again, the first requirement is a sharp blade of suitable width, a 12mm (½") blade with 6 teeth to the inch will produce nice, smooth tenons. The bandsaw fence must be checked to ensure that it is perfectly square to the table. If the fence is not square to the table, fit a wooden subfence to it (either bolted or screwed) and check again. Any slight deviation from 90 degrees can be corrected with a couple of shavings with a hand plane. If the tenons are to be cut in wide material such as might be needed for door rails, a tall fence should be fitted, again, checking to ensure that it is perfectly square to the table. The best way to tackle the actual cutting is to cut the shoulders first. Failure to follow this practice may result in the blade getting jammed in the cut, making it difficult or even impossible to withdraw it. If the bandsaw is very accurate it is possible, using a fine blade and a crosscut/mitre slide, to cut the tenon shoulders with the bandsaw.

CUTTING CIRCULAR DISCS WITH THE BANDSAW
Some makes of bandsaw have circle cutting

attachments supplied as part of the machine's equipment, others offer it as an optional accessory. It is quite easy to make a simple circle cutting device using a piece of ply (at least 12mm thick) with a sharpened panel pin placed at the correct radius and in line with the front of the sawblade. A more elaborate device with an adjustable radius is shown in the illustration. (*Fig. 17*)

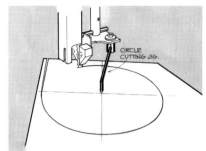

FIG. 17

The Circular Saw

CUTTING SHEET MATERIAL
Many woodworkers find that when cutting sheet materials they cannot achieve a satisfactory finish. This particularly applies to open-grained plywoods and plastic laminate. What actually does the damage is the back or up-running part of the sawblade. The problem can be overcome by using a sharp medium-to-fine tooth TCT blade which is adjusted so that it is cutting about
6-8mm above the top surface of the material. Some sort of hold-down device is useful when making this type of cut.

CUTTING REBATES AND GROOVES
Those who do not possess a spindle moulder or router for grooving and rebating frequently carry out these operations on the circular saw. There is nothing wrong with this practice providing certain precautions are taken.

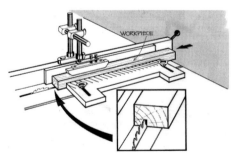

FIG. 18

Always use some sort of hold-down device when rebating or grooving, and a lateral spring is also a good additional safeguard. These devices can sometimes be obtained from the machine manufacturers, but failing

this, effective springs can be made in the workshop
from ply or MDF. (*Fig. 18, previous page*)

DEEP CUTTING ON THE CIRCULAR SAW

Very few woodworkers have not been tempted, at some
time, to try and work a machine beyond its true
capacity. It is true to say that whatever machine you
have there always comes a time when a bit more
capacity is needed. In the case of the circular saw this
can lead to the very dangerous practice of double
cutting, or "going twice", as it is sometimes called. For
example, it is necessary to deep cut a piece of timber
150mm (6") wide on a saw with a maximum depth of
cut of 75mm (3"). To do this the crown guard is
removed, the first cut made and the material turned
over for the second cut. This is an extremely hazardous
method of working, as with no guard the workpiece can
be flung back in the operator's face. The rule, therefore,
is never use a circular saw without a crown guard or
suitable alternative method of guarding.

A problem that is often encountered when ripping
certain timbers, mainly hardwoods, is "binding". This is
when the kerf made by the sawblade is closed due to
the cut releasing tensions in the timber. If this is only
slight the riving knife will suffice to overcome the
problem, but if it is severe a good tip is to have a
hardwood wedge hung up near the out-feed side of the
saw so that an assistant can insert this wedge at the
appropriate time, allowing the cut to be made without
difficulty.

BLADE SIZES ON CIRCULAR SAWS

Most circular saws run at a fixed speed, variable speed
saws being fairly rare. The factor that governs the safe
running speed of a saw is its periphery speed. This is
the lineal distance one sawtip will travel in a minute. It
has been established that 3000 metres (10,000 ft) per
minute is about right. Thus a 250mm (10") blade

running at 3000rpm is about right. The rule of thumb is that no sawblade used should be smaller than six tenths of the size of the largest blade the machine will take. For a 250mm (10") saw this will be 150mm (6"). The effect of using a blade too small will be a tendency for it to "snatch" rather than cut smoothly, which could be hazardous for the operator.

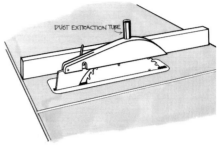

FIG. 19

DUST EXTRACTION ON THE SAWBENCH

Dust is a constant problem when using woodworking machinery and it is certainly good working practice to have extraction fitted to any circular saw. Normal extraction is underneath the sawblade and this is usually found to be insufficient if very dusty material such as MDF is being cut. A good tip is to fit a tube, of suitable diameter, in the top of the crown guard. A hose can then be connected to a vacuum extractor (or a domestic vacuum cleaner if it's a short run). This will pick up the dust from the top of the blade and ensure dust-free cutting. (*Fig. 19*)

PUSHSTICKS

Every circular saw should be equipped with at least one properly made pushstick hung in such a position that it is always readily to hand. A better idea is to have two or three of varying sizes to suit the work in hand. It is sometimes necessary to use two pushsticks when cutting small pieces, one to hold the workpiece against the fence and the other to hold it to the saw table.

The Radial Arm Saw

REPEAT CUTTING USING A STOP

Although many use the radial arm saw in a variety of ways its prime function is accurate crosscutting. Once accurately set up for this purpose it is a priceless asset

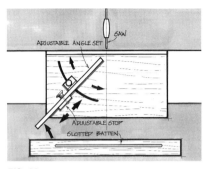

FIG. 20

in any workshop. For repeat cuts, a stop is fitted on the left-hand-side of the saw so that the material is fed in from the right. Thus the workpiece is held securely when the cut is being made. Cutting with the radial arm saw should be smooth and steady – not too fast – and the blade should be pushed right back at the completion of the cut.

ANGLE CUTTING WITH THE RADIAL ARM SAW
Angled cuts can be made with the radial arm saw by moving the arm to the desired angle. The disadvantage is that once a number of angle cuts have been made the fence is virtually destroyed and a new fence has to be fitted. Furthermore, once the arm is moved from the 90 degree position, despite the fact that positive stops are provided, some adjustment is usually needed to obtain perfect accuracy.

A partial solution to this problem is to leave the arm in the 90 degree position and use a batten set to the correct angle. If desired, a device can easily be made to produce a variety of angles. (*Fig. 20*)

THE RUN OFF TABLE
For those working single handed, a run off table at the rear of the sawbench is really essential. For those in an industrial situation it is a legal requirement, as the regulations state that such a table must be provided so that any person assisting a sawyer must be at least 1200mm (4ft) from the up-running part of the sawblade. Such a table can easily be made to fit in position when required.

JIGS & HOLDING DEVICES

Angled mortise jigs

When cutting angled mortise and tenon joints, first cut a piece of ply or MDF to the exact angle required and use that as a jig to hold the timber in both the mortiser and the radial arm when cutting the shoulders. Use it one way round for the first shoulder, then reverse it for the second.

Deep template cuts

When routing shapes using a template and a guide bushing, often the cutter may be too short to cut right through the timber. If this is the case and no long bit is available, cut as deep as the cutter will allow, around the shape. Use a jigsaw to cut away the waste, following the centre of the router cut. Change to a straight, bearing-guided bit, and trim back to the line using the bearing to follow the edge of the first cut.

Cheap bench hold-down

Cut a hole in the middle of your bench top just large enough to pass the bottom arm of a speed cramp through. Use the cramp as a quick hold-down when working on pieces of wood that need to be cramped to the workbench. Don't forget to use a softening block between cramp and workpiece.

Cramping blocks

Make softening blocks for sash/cramps out of offcuts of
timber. Cut a slot in one side to slip over the bar, so that
the block stays in place in use. Always keep a small box
of these handy when gluing up. Similarly, drill a circular
hole halfway into a small block, just snug enough to fit
over the heads of ordinary clamps without falling off.

Folding Wedge Cramps

To hold a piece of board or timber securely whilst
routing or sanding the top face, first nail, screw or
clamp two parallel, thin slats to the bench on either
side of the workpiece. Secure the piece by using folding
wedges between timber and slats. Multiple pieces can
be quickly exchanged with a few light taps from a
hammer, and the entire top face is left exposed for
working on. Ensure that the wedges, etc., are thinner
than the workpiece. This method works well with odd
shaped pieces or circular work.

Bench hook

Screw and glue 2 x 1 timber strips to the top of one end
of a 6 x 1 board and the bottom or the other end, to
form a bench hook that holds timber steady whilst
crosscutting by hand. Mitre guides can be cut into the
top strip for extra versatility. For more control, hold the
hook in a vice.

Router jig for trimming edging

Timber edging strips on ply or veneered boards can be
trimmed flush with a simple sub-base attachment to
the router. Bolt the router to the end of a thin piece of
plywood with the end under the router cut just short of
the cutting arc of the cutter-bit used. Sit the assembly
on the workpiece and plunge the router to just skim the

top of the board. Set the fence so that the cutter trims the edging strip. Ensure that the router bit is suitable for bottom cutting. (*Fig. 1*)

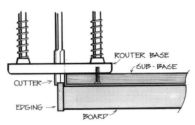

FIG. 1

False vice cheeks

Make two L-shaped false cheeks out of wood to sit in the vice. Cut various shaped, matching slots and grooves in either face, to hold small items, like dowels or handles, for working on. (*Fig. 2*)

Thicknessing Jig

Thicknessers do not like planing very thin pieces of timber and often are unable to plane less than 10mm. A false table can be made to raise the workpiece to the cutters so that thicknessing to even 1mm is possible. Cut a piece of board – melamine faced chipboard is great, otherwise waxed MDF or ply will do – as long as the table, and screw a batten to the underside of the rear end. Simply drop into place: the stop will hold the jig firmly in place as wood is passed over it.

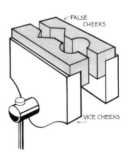

FIG. 2

Dowel hook

Plane a deep 45 degree bevel along one edge of a piece of 2 or 3 x 1. Cut the timber in half and glue the bevelled edges together so that the final piece has a V-shaped groove running down it. This will hold dowels when sawing and prevent them slipping. For further versatility, glue a lengthwise strip of timber to the underside to hold in the vice. A sawcut across the jig will help keep a saw accurate, and stops can be added to one end to enable multiple lengths to be cut to precisely the same size.

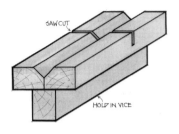

FIG. 3

Sash cramp vice

To hold a piece of wood lengthwise for working on – e.g. planing or tapering – first fix a sash cramp in the vice jaws. Timber can then be secured between the sash cramp heads, leaving unrestricted access to the edges. (*Fig. 3*)

Stickytape holdfasts

Keep a supply of masking tape, double-sided carpet tape and ducting tape handy. The double-sided tape can be used to fix workpieces to templates for routing, etc. The others are handy for holding small glued joints.

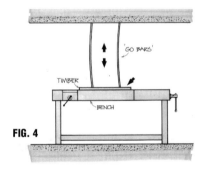

FIG. 4

Go Bars

If you have a low ceiling in your workshop, keep a set of thin (9 x 20mm) strips of springy timber, just longer than the distance from worktop to ceiling. These can be sprung into place to hold thin sheets of timber to the bench, or even for cramping pieces together when there are no G-cramps available. (*Fig. 4*)

FIG. 5

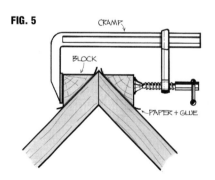

Mitre clamping blocks

It is quite difficult to clamp mitre joints on boxes, etc. One method that helps is to cut small right-angled triangular blocks and lightly glue the long side to the end of each side of the workpiece with a scrap of paper between block and timber. When dry use the blocks as a purchase point for cramps. After the glue has set on the workpiece, knock off the blocks along the paper joint and sand clean. (*Fig. 5*)

Featherboards

A featherboard is a simple method of holding timber tight against a fence on a tablesaw or router table. Make a series of diagonal cuts, close together, along the side of a piece of plywood or MDF resembling a feather. Firmly cramp the board into a position that will hold the workpiece but allow easy movement, ensuring that the fingers flow away from the direction of feeding. When the board has lost a few fingers, throw away and make new ones. Featherboards fixed to the fence will also act as a hold-down. (*Fig. 6*)

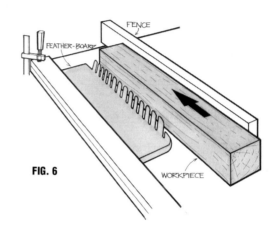

FIG. 6

Small cramps

Sometimes small workpieces can be too small for conventional cramps. It is not necessary to use excessive pressure when gluing up, and in these circumstances items such as butterfly clips, wooden pegs, and even elastic bands will be sufficient to hold two pieces in contact while the glue sets.

Non-slip jig surfaces

A thin piece of sandpaper glued to the face of a jig helps provide a non-slip surface for the workpiece to sit against. Don't forget to allow for the thickness of this when designing your jig. Similarly, a touch of wax will help ease a sticking one.

Tufnol jigs

Cheap and quick jigs and templates can be made of plywood or MDF but for long-lasting ones that will take a lot of wear, use perspex or tufnol (available from any plastics supplier). These can be cut and shaped just as easily as the wooden variety. Remember to label them with any useful information for the future.

Keep old jigs

Don't throw out a specific jig or template after use. You never know when it might come in handy again. Drill a hole and hang it on a nail somewhere out of the way. Mark router templates with the size of the cutter and template bush that you used, and any other useful information.

FIG. 7

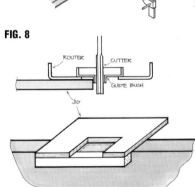

Convex cramp extension

It is often difficult to get a cramp onto the middle of a wide board, for example, when gluing up a large carcass. Take a thickish piece of timber, long enough to span the width of the board, and plane a slight convex curve on one edge. Using a cramp on either end will cause extra pressure to be applied in the middle, just where it's wanted. (*Fig. 7*)

FIG. 8

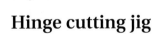

Hinge cutting jig

Use a router to speed up cutting hinge recesses in doors. Select a suitable bit and guide bush combination and make a template to fit the chosen hinge size. Screw a batten under the template to act as a fence that can be

clamped to the door, and adjust the depth of cut to the size of the hinge. Rout the door and the batten together, so that the correct plunge depth can be easily established on the next set-up. Square-off the hinge recess afterwards with a sharp chisel.
(*Fig. 8 previous page*)

Table saw jig for small timbers

FIG. 9

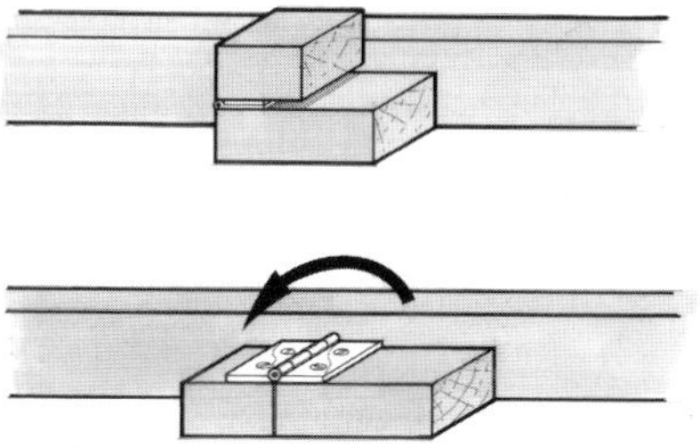

Make carrying cradles to hold small pieces of irregularly shaped timber for passing through a table saw or router. Place the timber on a large piece of plywood with the cutting line parallel to one edge of the ply. Nail or screw small battens around the workpiece to confine it, and secure with hold-downs if necessary. Set fence to correct distance and pass complete arrangement through the saw.

It is often necessary, when cutting lots of identical pieces to length with a stop on a radial arm saw, to cut both ends of the timber. Cut a couple of inches off a short piece of 2 x 1, and join it back to the timber with a hinge. Clamp the 2 x 1 to the saw-fence so that the end of the small block forms the desired stop. Flip up the hinged piece and make the first cut. Then drop the block and make the second one. For accuracy, ensure there is no free-play in the hinge as it pivots.
(*Fig. 9*)

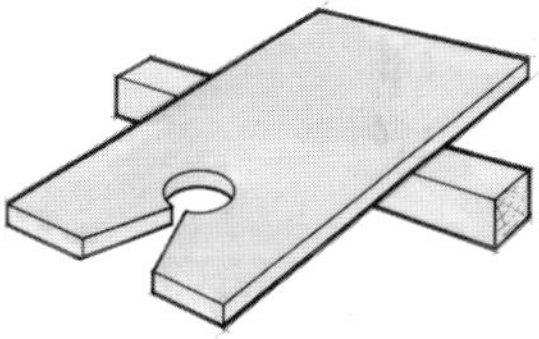

FIG. 10

Work support for coping saw

An old way of supporting a piece of timber whilst cutting shapes with a coping saw – or a modern jigsaw – is as follows. Take a piece of 12" x 7" plywood and screw a short 2 x 2 batten across the width near the middle. Drill a 50mm (2") diameter hole just forward of this, and connect it to the front end with a V-shaped notch. After cramping the batten in the vice, the board will help support the work whilst leaving a free central area for the sawblade and allowing the timber to be moved around. (*Fig. 10, previous page*)

Clean work surfaces

Keep all cramp heads, vice cheeks and work surfaces clean of chips when holding work. Loose bits can get trapped and pressed into the timber, causing scarring and scratches, that will require more sanding to remove.

FIG. 11

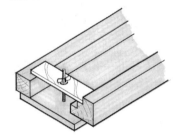

Protect wood from staining

Certain woods, especially oak, will react against iron when wet, and cause staining. It is therefore important to ensure that no glue comes into contact with both the wood and clamps when gluing up. Wipe excess off immediately if possible. Slips of paper placed under the sash-clamps will act as a barrier in situations such as jointing up large panels where it is not always possible to clean up.

Homemade jig clamps

It is worth fitting often-used jigs and templates, for carrying wood through a moulder or saw, with a clamping system. If you cannot afford to buy hold-downs, make your own. Drill a couple of long bolts up through the base, past the workpiece, and through a metal or wooden plate, finishing with washers and wingnuts. Place the workpiece under one end of the plate and a stepped block under the other, to balance it, and tighten nut to clamp to base. (*Fig. 11*)

Wax jigs

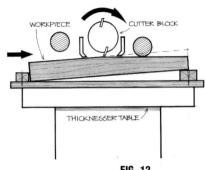

FIG. 12

A little wax on the running surfaces of a jig will ensure it moves easily against machined surfaces, without sticking. This can be especially useful where the timber is carried through cradle-type jigs in a thicknesser for shaping. Pine is often the worst timber for sticking because of the resins contained within the wood.

Taper jig for thicknesser

FIG. 13

Perhaps the easiest method of tapering timber is with a thicknesser. Make a simple jig to hold the stock and carry it through the machine. Screw a stop to the back end of a length of board, slightly longer than the piece to be tapered, and a shim, equal to the amount of taper, to the other end. This should be placed under the leading end of the timber. Place the workpiece on the jig and pass through the thicknesser. If the wood bends, insert extra (proportional) shims underneath, along its length. (*Fig. 12*)

Simple cam clamp for jig

FIG. 14

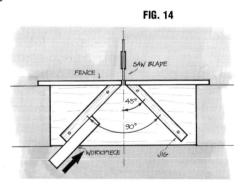

A simple cam clamp will often suffice to secure a piece of timber into a jig. (*Fig. 13*). Make one by shaping a long triangular shape in half-inch ply with a semi-circular base. Drill an off-centre pivot point and screw to appropriate part of jig through it. Apply pressure to long end to clamp. Ensure that cam is positioned so that it tightens, rather than loosens its hold against the force of the machine cutter.

Radial arm saw mitre jig

Instead of resetting a radial arm saw to cut mitres, make a jig so that the blade remains at a 90 degree angle. Screw a batten onto a baseboard at an accurate 45 degree to the edge, then place a set square against this and hold it firm to align a second batten at 90 degrees to the first. Position the board against the saw's fence and cut one mitre on one side, and its mate on the other. As long as the jig is accurate, any small change in the angle of the blade will be compensated for, and the joint will be a true 90 degrees.

(*Fig. 14, previous page*)

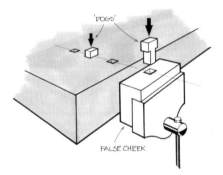

FIG. 15

Dowels as softening blocks

When jointing large panels with sash cramps, slight movement in the cramp heads can cause thin boards to buckle slightly. Use pieces of dowel, the same diameter as the thickness of the boards, as softening blocks. This will ensure that any flexing of the heads on the bars will still exert the correct directional pressure to the middle of each board and keep the panels flat. As an extra precaution, lightly sandwich and cramp the ends of the panels between two battens.

Simple bench dogs

A system of dogs for holding wood is a standard fitment of many traditional benches. (*Fig. 15*). Make a simple version for extending the reach of your vice by cutting a series of mortises through the bench top at right angles to the centre of the vice. Fit a false cheek to the moving part of the vice with a corresponding mortise in it. Cut several shouldered blocks to fit the mortises, enabling them to protrude by about half an inch. Keep them handy and fit for use as required.

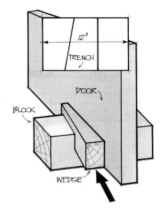

FIG. 16

Holding thin strips of wood

If you have no vice it can be difficult to hold a piece of thin timber upright to plane the edges. Make a v-cut in the end of a piece of thick plywood or timber, with one side at right angles to the end. Screw or cramp this to the bench top as a stop. Hold the timber to be planed in place in the V with a wedge. Cut the pointed end off the wedge to ensure that it holds the wood securely. (*Fig. 16*)

Vacuum clamp

If you have a dust extractor or vacuum cleaner in the workshop, try making a vacuum clamp for holding workpieces. Construct an open top box approx 250 x 250 x 50mm (10 x 10 x 2") and fix it down to a convenient surface. Line the top edges with a self-adhesive draught excluder strip and drill a hole in the side to accept the extractor nozzle. Place board on top and turn on extractor. The hold should be strong enough to hold work steady whilst routing mouldings, etc.

Bigger sash cramps

Sash cramps have a habit of not being quite long enough for the job in hand. Two cramps can be cannibalised to make a longer one by removing the slicing heads and bolting the bars together through two sets of pinholes.

Shelf support jig

When making cupboards, it can be a hassle to measure and mark each hole for drilling moveable-pin shelf supports to the correct depth. Make a jig by marking out and drilling a length of batten with the necessary holes, and cramp this into place in the carcass. Drill through the end of a small scrap of wood, remove and trim to length, so that the drill bit protrudes just enough to cut to correct depth, allowing for the thickness of the jig. Drill holes and move jig to next location.

Cutting guide for circular saw

A powersaw can cut its own aligning guide as follows. Take a bit of ply or MDF, a little wider than the saw and long enough to act as a straight edge. Screw a straight piece of 2 x 1 to it, close to one edge. Clamp this construction down and cut along it with the saw, using the batten as a fence. The board can now be aligned to a cutting line, and, provided the saw is held tight to the fence, it will cut accurately to that line. Make sure the saw does not tilt when cutting.

Trammel jig for router

A trammel arm is invaluable for cutting circles with a router. If you don't have one, a simple piece of ply will help cut small circles. Mark a straight line down the middle of a triangular-ish bit of thin ply. Fix the router base to the bottom end of the ply with the centre of the cutter accurately placed over the line. Measure desired radius of cut along the line from the cutter and drill a hole. Use this as a pivot point for a nail or a screw, which can be fixed to the underside of the workpiece.

Router crosscut jig

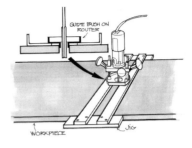

A router can perform accurate cross cuts
with the aid of a guide bush and a jig. Lay
two pieces of 3 x 1 about 7" apart and
parallel, and screw another bit on top and
at right angles to both. Place the desired
guide bush against this piece at one end
and use as a spacer to position and fix a

FIG. 17

fourth timber alongside it. Repeat at other end to
complete square so that bush runs snugly between the
two. Use base pieces as fences, and cramp top bars to
workpiece checking that they do not foul the router.
(*Fig. 17*)

Cheap sash clamps

Sash clamps are very expensive, so try making your own
with bought-in clamp heads and a length of wood,
drilled with a series of anchor-pin holes. Take care with
this, as badly centred holes can affect the smooth
running of the clamps. The main advantage of these
clamps is that you can keep a variety of lengths all
using the same heads. Remember though, that old
adage: you can never have enough clamps.

Making templates

Accuracy is vital when making templates for routing.
Where possible, cut the various parts using a router,
with straightedges and trammelbars to guide the cuts. If
necessary make templates to cut templates.

Mitre box

One of the most essential jigs for the bench is the mitre
box, for cutting accurate 45 degree (or other) mitres by
hand. Screw two short bits of 4 x 1 to either side of a
piece of 2 x 1, ensuring the undersides are all dead

flush. Mark a 45 degree angle across the top of both boards, square down and cut down to the base board. Cut an opposite angle, similarly, alongside. Use the same saw for cutting the stock to ensure the blade doesn't wander. When worn, discard and remake.

Shooting board

A shooting board will allow the edges and ends of timbers to be planed square. Make one by fixing a straight piece of board down onto another wider one to form a wide rebate. Groove and screw an end-stop square to one end of the top piece and plane flush with the edge. Use by holding the timber to be squared against the stop and rest a plane (on its side) on the lower board. Set the blade finely and squarely, and let it follow the straightedge.

Stopping router breakout

Routing the ends of timber on a router table will cause breakout unless the cut is backed up as it exits the cutter. Cut a square end on a piece of timber, the same thickness as the stock, and make a handle that can be screwed to its top. Pass the workpiece through the router, held tight against the backing block, until the cutter has cut into the latter. It may help to fix a projecting batten to the top of the block to act as a hold-down on the timber. Save the handle for other work.

Mitre template

When making mortise and tenon frames with moulded interior edges, it will be necessary to mitre their joins. Perhaps the easiest way is to use a mitre template, made by cutting a deep rebate into a length of hardwood 2 x 2 and trimming either end to 45 degrees. Hold this firmly over the moulded edge and using the angled face to guide a sharp chisel, pare back to the shoulder line. Use the opposite end to cut the corresponding angle.

Edge gluing with speed cramps

Gluing timber edging to veneered board can often take more long cramps than are available. In this situation, speed cramps or G-cramps can be employed. Fix a cramp onto the board a couple of centimetres from the edge and tap a timber wedge between the bar and the edging to hold the timber firmly in place. More pressure can be exerted by cutting one face of the wedge slightly concave, and placing this face against the edging.

45 degree jig for thicknesser

An easily made cradle will let a thicknesser put a 45 degree champfer on a piece of timber, or even make octagonal section stock. Cut a length of 2 x 2 diagonally down the middle and plane the sawn faces accurately to 45 degrees. Then, screw both to a larger baseplate so that their angled faces form a long V-groove. This can now be cramped to the thicknesser table to present timber at an angle to the cutters. If the surfaces are not as smooth as you would like some wax will help the stock slide easily. Once you have mastered this, you will find that a slight adaptation will allow other angles to be planed just as easily. (*Fig. 18*)

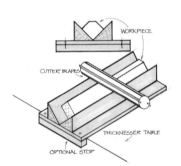

FIG. 18

Screw wood down

Sometimes the quickest way to hold a workpiece on a bench for cutting or routing is simply to screw it down. Just make sure that the screws are in a part of the timber that will be subsequently cut away or hidden, such as a joint. Don't forget to place them away from the path of the saw or router though.

Batten fences

When routing a rebate or moulding into a large number of pieces of timber, it can be rather tedious to put each piece into a vice to hold it. All that is necessary is a simple back fence – thinner than the stock – nailed to the benchtop, with a stop to prevent the timber moving back under the router. If the stock is thin it may be necessary to position it close to the edge of the bench so that the router fence does not foul on the edge.

Router T-square

A homemade square will help a router cut housings and dadoes. Screw two pieces of 76mm (3") wide ply together to form a T and check for square. This is cramped to the workpiece to form a straightedge guide. If the first cut with the router is carried through the end of the T-square, the resulting groove will act as an accurate index mark for subsequent cuts. Two identical squares, one on either side of the workpiece, can be set to guide the router, when the dado width is greater than the available cutters.

Bandsaw wedges

Wedges are time-consuming to cut by hand. Make a jig to cut them on the bandsaw which is by far the simplest, most accurate and the safest way. Cut the wedge shape out of the long edge of a rectangular piece of ply or MDF and set the bandsaw fence so that the blade just skims the ply. Cross-cut some timber to the correct wedge length, press one corner into the jig cut-out and pass both pieces through the saw. Reverse the workpiece and cut again. It can pay to cut lots at one go and keep until needed.

Circle jig for bandsaw

Make a quick jig to cut a circle on
the bandsaw. Screw a thin batten, to
run in the saw's mitre fence groove,
to the underside of a piece of ply.
Pass this arrangement through the
saw to trim off waste and square a
line across the middle of the board
from this edge. Arrange a stop, so
that the sawblade is in line with this
pencil line. Put a small nail through
the board at the appropriate point
along the line to act as a centre
pivot for the circle. Place the timber square on the
pivot, advance the jig into the saw and turn. (*Fig. 19*)

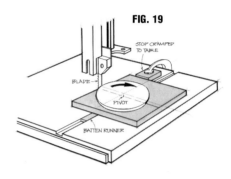

FIG. 19

Tenon saw gauge

It is handy to have a depth gauge on the tenon saw
when cutting the shoulders of housings. This can be
made by cutting two thin fillets of timber, slightly
longer than the length of the saw blade, and drilling a
hole in each end of both pieces. Put a small bolt and
wingnut through each end to bolt the pieces together
around the saw. To use, set the gauge parallel to the
teeth, at the correct distance, tighten the nuts, and cut
the shoulder until the teeth no longer bite.

Marking out for machines

To speed up work, remember that when cutting joints,
etc., using machine set-ups, it is not necessary to mark
out every identical piece of timber. For example, when
cutting tenon shoulders on a radial arm saw, cut all
timbers so that one stop can be used to cut each
shoulder, whatever the length of timber. Accuracy is
essential at the cross-cutting stage though, or else all
subsequent cutting will suffer.

RESTORATION

Staining & Polishing

WATER STAINS
Use on bare or new wood, available in various colours.
OIL STAINS
Use for adjusting the colour of a polished surface to match an existing colour.
SPIRIT STAINS
Use for colouring out patches with thin polish.
PIGMENTS
Use with water or polish to obtain required colour.
BLEACHES
For changing surface colour, available as a two pack.
ACETIC ACID
Use for neutralising a bleached surface.
APPLYING STAIN TO A FLAT SURFACE
Use a cloth and always follow the grain.
APPLYING STAIN TO CURVED SURFACES
Use a brush, wipe off excess with a cloth.
STAINING A NEW SURFACE
Wet surface to raise grain, re-sand prior to applying stain as above.
STRIPPING
Use a liquid stripper, apply with a brush, remove excess with a cloth or 0000 wire wood, neutralise with meths.
STRIPPING CURVED SURFACES
Use a toothbrush for removing old varnish.
POLISHING A FLAT SURFACE
Use a polishing rubber.
POLISHING RUBBERS
Made from pure cotton with either wadding or cotton wood insert, twisted to form a mouse shape.
STORAGE
Keep polish rubbers in an airtight jar to prevent them

drying out.

POLISH FOR USE IN RUBBERS
This can easily be kept in old washing-up bottles.

POLISHING MOP
Use to apply polish to curved or moulded surfaces.

POLISHING MOPS
Can be purchased from good art shops or polish suppliers, available with squirrel or zorrino bristles.

STORAGE
To prevent drying out keep brushes in a jar suspended in meths.

SUSPENDING MOP
Insert a panel pin in the handle to enable the brush to rest on the edge of the jar.

IRREGULAR USE
Cover jar and top with clingfilm to prevent evaporation.

WIRE WOOL
Available in various grades.

0000 WIRE WOOL
Use for cutting back a surface for the next application.

INK MARKS
Apply oxalic acid, neutralise with water.

WATER MARKS
Apply reviver with a cloth or 0000 wire wool for slight abrasion.

GREASE STAINS
Apply washing soda.

HOT AIR GUN
Used for speeding up drying times of water stains.

FILLING SPLITS
Use a soft filler stick available in various colours.

FILLING DENTS, HOLES
Use a hard shellac filler stick, available in various colours, melt before use.

Wax Polishing

WAX POLISH
Available in different makes and colours. All waxes

contain beeswax, paraffin wax or carnuaba wax.

LIGHT TIMBERS
Satinwood, walnut, etc., use a light-coloured wax.

DARK TIMBERS
Mahogany, ebony, etc., use a dark-coloured wax.

FLAT SURFACES
Apply wax in a circular motion with either cotton waste or a soft cloth.

CURVED OR MOULDED SURFACES
Apply wax with a shoe brush.

FINISH
Use a mutton cloth or soft cloth to remove excess wax. For best finish use a duster to final wax.

CARNUABA WAX
Can be used when turning to achieve finished result.

SPRAY POLISHES
Avoid on antique furniture: they contain silicone and may leave white deposits in the grain.

DRAWER RUNNERS
These can be waxed with paraffin wax to ease use.

WOODWORM
Treat with either an injector or paint brush.

WOODWORM TREATMENT
Treat bottoms and backs of carcasses, avoiding inside drawers and polished surfaces.

HOLES IN POLISHED SURFACES
Use a soft wax which can be applied to holes with a soft cloth.

Repairs – Equipment Required

HACKSAW
Cutting metal fittings, screws and timber which may contain hidden nails.

JUNIOR HACKSAW
The fine blade is ideal for cutting inlays and bandings.

HACKSAW BLADE
Use in place of a toothing plane to key surface prior to veneering.

RUBBER MALLET
Use for dismantling, avoids damage to surface.
SCRATCH STOCK
Handmade tool used for reproducing mouldings
(*Fig. 1*)
UPHOLSTERY SPRINGS
Cut up and use for holding irregular shapes
while glue dries.
CLOTHES PEGS
Use for applying light pressure whilst glue dries.
TOURNIQUET
Rope tied round two legs to act as a cramp
whilst glue dries.
BELT CRAMP
Use for cramping up chairs or awkward shapes.
JUBILEE CLIP
Apply to split leg to enable a dowel to be drilled easier.
MASKING TAPE
For extra pressure, twist to form a butterfly shape, for
holding mouldings, stringing etc.
GUMMED TAPE
Use for holding joints in veneer marquetry prior to
laying veneer. Remove after use.
VENEER PINS
Use for holding stringing in place while waiting for the
glue to dry.
ANIMAL OR SCOTCH GLUE
Use for all types of restoration work, jointing,
veneering, etc.
SYRINGE
Use for applying glue to bubbles in veneer, loose joints,
etc.
HOT BLOCK
Heat MDF block and use with glue to lay veneer,
bubbles, etc.
IRON
Hot iron, used for ironing veneer flat after laying.
PALLET KNIFE
Use for inserting glue into joints, veneer, etc.

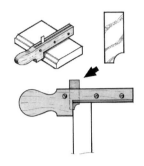

FIG. 1

LAYING LEATHER
To achieve a neat edge, a brass castor can be used to press the leather down close to the veneer.

OLD LEATHER
Revive old or worn leather with a hide cream; rub into surface.

AGEING NEW BRASS
Key surface with 0000 wire wool, place brass on a timber block in a sealed container with ammonia to achieve required finish.

CLEANING BRASS
Use a burnishing cream with a soft cloth or 0000 wire wool.

Repairs

ROUTER
Use for removing excess wood when splicing or repairing veneer.

VENEER
When repairing veneer try to use timber of a similar age and colour.

POLISHED SURFACES
When cramping use newspaper between the block and the surface so you avoid causing any damage to the polish.

FIG. 2

HARDBOARD
Use for making templates and patterns.

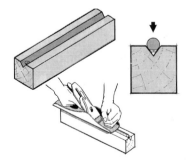

WOODEN PLUGS
Cut end grain of timber and use a simple box as shown. Rotate to achieve the required result. (*Fig. 2*)

SCREWS AND NAILS
Remove with a homemade drill as illustrated. (*Fig. 3, see over the page*)

SPLICING LEGS
The best method is marked with a tick; avoid the method marked with a cross. (*Fig. 4, see over the page*)

FIG. 3

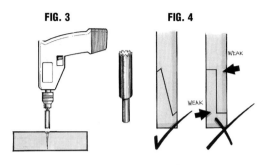

FIG. 4

SPLICING CURVED LEGS
The best method is marked with a tick; avoid the method marked with a cross. (*Fig. 5*)

TURNED LEGS
Cut off broken section and dowel on replacement part.

BROKEN TENONS
Fit false tenons as illustrated. (*Fig. 6*)

FIG. 5

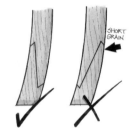

CRAMPING CURVED ITEMS
Make a block as shown in illustration. (*Fig. 7*)

CUTTING CROSSBANDING
Put masking tape on end of veneer to stop splitting.

SEAT FRAMES
Construct using a dowelled joint in place of mortise and tenon.

CURVED WORK
A surf-form can be used to remove excess waste.

ELECTRIC DRILL
Use a flap disk for sanding curved surfaces.

FIG. 6

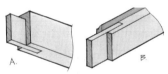

DRY CLAMPING
Always dry cramp to check that joints are a good fit prior to gluing.

EXCESS GLUE
Always wipe off glue after cramping with a damp cloth, this saves time and will prevent possible damage to polished surfaces.

FIG. 7

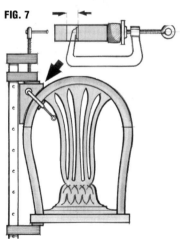

CHECK DIAGONALS
Always check the diagonals to see if they are square. If not, then they can be altered while the glue is still flexible, if you catch them in time.

DESIGNING & MAKING FURNITURE

If you are designing a new chair (for example) there is no point in over-engineering the prototype. You learn nothing from making it too strong. It is best to make a modest structure in softwood so you can see where the weaknesses lie and then beef up the final design (e.g. make it perhaps 3mm stouter) using hardwood.

A common problem with tables (such as for pubs and restaurants) is that they often rock and spill liquids. The easy solution is to design a table which has three legs, not four!

FIG. 1

When designing try to empty your head of pre-conceptions about the way a piece should look or be made and start at the beginning by identifying the problems – asking a series of questions about form, function, material, techniques, etc. Often one problem can trigger the idea for a design, e.g. the problem with a lot of cabinets is that their handles let them down and bear little relation to the overall design. Try designing a cabinet which opens without the need for handles.

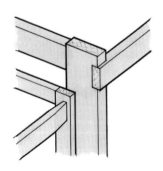

Try to stagger the joints on adjacent members to avoid breaking up essential fibres where strength is needed (*Fig. 1*). This opens up possibilities for interesting designs for chairs and tables in particular.

When designing furniture make pictorial "thumbnail" sketches to explore quickly and visualize the possibilities. Solving all the problems on a draughtsman's board is rigid and unimaginative and seldom possible. Ideas can come in the workshop whilst handling materials and can often be scribbled on a scrap piece of wood at hand.

FIG. 2

A strong design idea often comes after a sustained, frustrating and intense mental effort to 'crack' the problem(s). You find you are getting nowhere and abandon the struggle. Curiously it is often after you have let go and you are thinking about something else that the solution suddenly presents itself as crystal clear! (*Fig. 2*)

A good piece of furniture design uses the material appropriately. If you use the material wrongly the design usually suffers – it is either not strong or durable enough or looks awkward. An obvious example is using dovetails on a chipboard or plywood carcass.

Over-decoration can be the disguise to poor design. Visual understatement which allows the economics and discipline of structure to dictate the form usually results in a more honest expression of material and techniques, both essential elements in good design. Designing is largely about observing and by observing nature in particular, many of the answers to design problems can be found.

Designing involves taking risks and making decisions. Taking risks involves accepting failure. Do not be afraid to put an idea to the test, as what is learned is a necessary building block towards becoming a confident designer. Confidence in your own ideas is what designing is about and the rewards are infinitely greater than purely copying others' ideas, which is the easier option.

There are countless examples of uncomfortable chairs around. It is actually quite easy to design a comfortable chair – you simply copy the data (back and seat rakes, lumbar support, etc.) from an existing comfortable chair! What is more difficult is designing a comfortable chair which is visually original, which looks great from all angles and is strong!

A good piece of furniture design asks questions and says something new and is relevant to the age we live in. Just creating something new for its own sake or to be different, or to be technically clever, is not enough today and only alienates modern design from what should be at its best a continuum of the best of tradition. Designing in a vacuum or with total freedom seldom brings results. A design 'brief' sets out the limitations or parameters, and curiously the tighter those are, the more creative the solutions often are. Making a chair from a limited length of 50mm x 25mm wood is a good example.

When designing in wood try and work within standard available sizes of materials. It is wasteful in materials and time not to do so.

When designing chests of drawers the way the drawer works and how it can be constructed with ease is a major consideration in the overall design concept. Traditional drawers are complex and time consuming to build and not entirely appropriate today (they often rattle in the summer and stick in the winter). Easy glide systems used in kitchen and office furniture systems can be the answer and this opens up the options for drawer construction in either solid wood or manufactured board.

If there is a technical/visual problem when designing, such as showing a screw or bolt head, either disguise it or make a visual feature of the problem, but avoid getting caught in-between. Why use a dovetail when a finger joint can look just as classy and may be quicker to make?

When designing you often start with a problem – a new chair concept can evolve from the specific problem such as how to achieve a curved back rail. Thinking laterally and investigating ways of achieving the back support that the curved piece makes but using a different means can open up the possibilities of an entirely different chair and you soon discover that you do not have to use the traditional solution. The English Windsor chair is a perfect example of how straight, easy-to-make back members create the necessary curve for the back. (*Fig. 3*)

FIG. 3

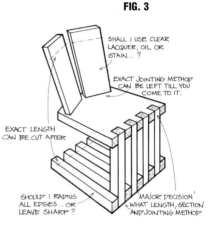

SHALL I USE CLEAR LACQUER, OIL OR STAIN... ?

EXACT JOINTING METHOD CAN BE LEFT TILL YOU COME TO IT.

EXACT LENGTH CAN BE CUT AFTER

SHOULD I RADIUS ALL EDGES... OR LEAVE SHARP ?

MAJOR DECISION WHAT LENGTH, SECTION AND JOINTING METHOD

FIG. 4

If you have designed and built a chair prototype and your eye has become so familiar with its form that you are beginning to lose a critical appraisal of it, try using a large mirror and you will curiously see the object in a fresh light. This is particularly useful for achieving those harmonious proportions so important to a well designed piece of furniture, and in particular, to a chair. (*Fig. 4*)

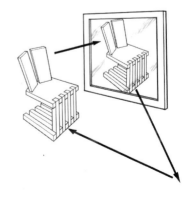

FIG. 5

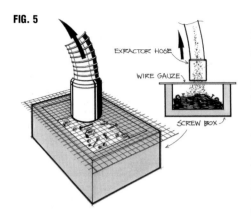

EXTRACTOR HOSE

WIRE GAUZE

SCREW BOX

Solve the major technical and aesthetic problems on paper first and then worry about details as you go along, depending on how the piece shapes up.

Furniture Making

Protect your workpiece during making by mounting it on a soft blanket or sheet of latex rubber on the bench.

One of the problems of storing screws, etc., in boxes or trays in the workshop is that they get filled with dust and debris. Try placing a fine gauze over the top of the box and use a dust-extractor hose to take away the dust, shaking the box as you do it. (*Fig. 5*)

FIG. 6

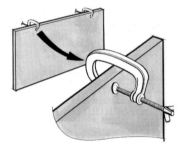

When trying to heave a large 8 x 4 sheet of plywood or chipboard single handed, especially lifting to a height, try placing two 150mm (6") G clamps on the sheet and use them as handles. (*Fig. 6*)

It is often better to work to a marked line even when using some power tools and machines. For instance, when ripping on the bandsaw the fence is not always a guarantee of a parallel line and when cross-cutting on a radial arm saw a squared line is the most accurate to work to.

Fig. 7

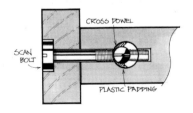

CROSS DOWEL

SCAN BOLT

PLASTIC PADDING

When using KD fittings (*Fig. 7*) such as scan bolts, in order to relocate the screw thread, a spot of epoxy glue or plastic padding bedding the cross dowel solves the problem of

FIG. 8

realignment every time.

Keep the wood as long as you can for as long as possible.

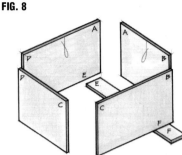

Try using a biro instead of a pencil for marking out. It is bold and clear with a consistently defined point, unlike a pencil which blunts as it draws and often does not show up on the wood. Any surplus biro marks can be easily planed or sanded off. A biro leaks very rarely. If it does, throw it away!

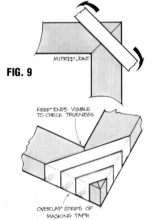

FIG. 9

Always use code marks (A, B, C, etc.) on different parts of a job. (*Fig. 8*)

When copying lengths and other repeat marking out operations, use the back of some glasspaper or similar stout card and use two pencil marks. Using a ruler each time increases the chance of mistakes.

Masking tape is an excellent clamping method for light work such as mitred frames. Use the stretchiness of the tape and always pull perpendicular to the glue line. The more tape you apply the greater the strength. But don't leave it on for days afterwards as it can lift the grain. (*Fig. 9*)

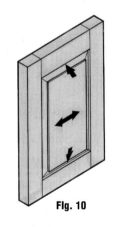

FIG. 11

Fig. 10

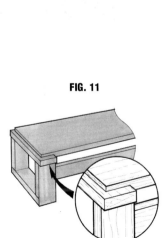

Use Cascamite for gluing dovetail joints and other lengthy assemblies. It has a longer pot of life than

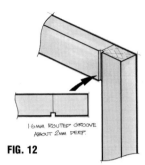

1.6MM ROUTED GROOVE
ABOUT 2MM DEEP.

FIG. 12

PVA and is less likely to go off while you are still clamping up.

When inserting loose panels in panelled frames glue a small blob at the centres so that the shrinkage occurs away from that fixed point evenly to either side. This avoids a gap showing on one side. (*Fig. 10, previous page*)

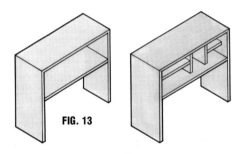

FIG. 13

A 'Danish shoulder' takes the eye away from likely timber movement on two adjacent pieces and emphasises the joint by visually separating it. Use a 1.6mm router cutter. (*Fig. 11, previous page*)

Avoid flush surfaces where possible in structures as it eases the making procedure and allows for timber movement. (*Fig. 12*)

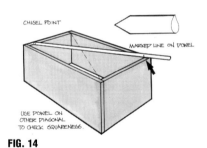

CHISEL POINT

MARKED LINE ON DOWEL

USE DOWEL ON
OTHER DIAGONAL
TO CHECK SQUARENESS.

FIG. 14

The traditional way to construct a complex carcass is to cut all joints first, which can make gluing difficult. Modern tools like the router and biscuit jointer allow some flexibility in further joint cutting after the main carcass has been glued up. (*Fig. 13*)

Squaring up a carcass can be done with some thin dowel rod, sharpened to a chisel at one end and checking diagonals to a marked line. (*Fig. 14*)

When planing large solid wood flat panels (e.g. table tops) use a jackplane across the grain first to break up the fibres and remove the bulk of the wood to get it flat and even, then plane with the grain to achieve the final finish. You minimize blisters this way!

MINIATURE WOOD WORK

Research & Planning

To make an accurate model in miniature you need to understand how the full-sized example was made originally, what it was made of and its proportions. Make sure that you are studying a genuine, accurate example and not someone else's vague interpretation! Failure to understand the detail will invariably result in a miniature which may be quite pleasing to the uninformed but will lack credibility.

For the beginner it is wise to stick to simple prototypes and then, as more experience is gained, more intricate and complex items can be constructed.

Since plans are seldom available for period items, and since photographs alone do not always show the full extent of detail required, the modeller needs really to see the real thing, be it a piece of furniture, a cart, a staircase or a building. He will be wise to look at examples in museums, stately homes and sale rooms and then follow this up with books and a study of Miller's antique guides.

Plans are available through specialist magazines and the MAP plans, booklets and other useful material will be found at the Model Engineer Exhibition and other similar shows.

Keeping a journal of progress through a long-term project with sketches, notes, photographs and measurements is useful and will become an invaluable reference. Sit comfortably in your armchair in the evening and with paper and pencil plan and list the next stage of the operation. It pays to be methodical and logical in your planning to avoid costly mistakes in time and money.

Kits

Do not be too proud to start with a kit. They are available for most modelling crafts and are a good way of introducing woodwork to youngsters.

Kits vary in quality and can be expensive, but they are a good way of starting your new hobby and should not be scorned.

The advantages are that all the material is usually included, the instructions should be clear and only very basic tools will be needed, although sometimes the quality of the wood supplied leaves much to be desired.

Scale

Scale and accuracy are very important and need to be checked regularly.

Make a home-made ruler so that every aspect of a model can be checked for accuracy of scale. A representative human figure in strong card or ply with moveable limbs can be a great aid in making sure proportions are right – if the mannikin is unable to go through the dolls' house door you know you are in trouble!

Keep your eyes open for an old school ruler in inches with 1/12" divisions; these are useful for the dolls' house enthusiast but such rulers are becoming hard to find.

A pair of Vernier callipers for inside, outside and depth measurements should be part of the miniaturist's equipment.

A pair of proportional dividers which can be set to increase or reduce scale are of particular value to the miniaturist.

Storage

Working in miniature, in a limited area, needs discipline and organisation. A bench cluttered with tools, shavings and small items of miniature woodwork will lead to frustration and possible injury.

Choose wooden or plastic boxes to store small tools and metal fittings in. Avoid metal tins which will soon rust.

Large, stacking, plastic storage boxes sold by DIY stores are good for storing small sections of wood and make it relatively easy to sort wood by type or size.

Strip wood can be stored in lengths of grey plastic drain pipe which is also obtainable from DIY stores. The tube can be plugged at the bottom with a glued-in wooden disc.

As you collect more and more plans, card templates and reference material, it becomes necessary to store such paper material safely indoors away from damp and mildew and one solution is to use clear A4 plastic pockets in a ring folder so that it will be easy to find what you are looking for.

Wood

When selecting which wood to use scale in grain is important and woods with large grain, although attractive in colour, look all wrong in scale furniture.

Use hardwoods such as box, lime, lemonwood, sycamore, holly, pear and ebony. These woods are all suitable for small scale work because they have fine grain, take a good finish, machine and drill well and will stain and glue. The woods listed are also good for turning and will give the crisp detail that the turner is looking for.

Stain and colour the wood until it represents oak, mahogany, antique pine or whatever wood the original was made in. Even if your model is to be painted, a fine grain wood will result in a smoother, more satisfying finish.

Plywood is normally used for making miniature buildings or dolls' houses and it is best to use birch-faced ply which comes in a wide range of thicknesses down to 1mm and is usually made from 5 laminations. You will probably need to go to a specialist timber supplier and it is expensive. Avoid cheap DIY type plywood which tends to splinter. Model shops should be able to supply small quantities but this is an expensive way of purchasing wood.

If large sheets are purchased, say 1.2 x 1.2m (4' x 4') or 2.4 x 2.4m (8' x 8') storage can be a problem as plywood will bend and warp if it is stored upright against a wall. It is recommended that large sheets be cut into smaller sheets and stored flat, for example, under a bed.

When varnishing or painting plywood remember to treat both sides equally to prevent warping.

Medium Density Fibreboard (MDF) does have a use in miniature woodwork as it is also good for building miniature buildings or dolls' houses and it is easily obtainable in a range of thicknesses from most DIY suppliers at a reasonable price. Again, it is wise to store it flat rather than upright and if it is to be painted or varnished both sides will need to be treated equally to prevent warping.

MDF produces a fine dust when it is cut or routed and a dust mask should be worn.

The surface of MDF is finished in the factory to a very high standard and therefore it is unwise to damage the surface during the construction process.

MDF has no grain but it is easy to cause splitting when screwing or nailing edges. Pilot holes should be drilled and positioned at least 70mm (2¾") from the corners of panels and spaced 150mm (6") apart to reduce the risk of splitting. The pilot hole should be 85 to 90% of the screw core diameter which, for a number 4 screw, would mean a pilot hole of 1.5mm. In the case of moulding pins drill the hole slightly smaller than the pin chosen.

Hand Tools

A good set of basic hand tools are needed for miniature woodwork, together with some more specialist tools.

When selecting your equipment go for good quality branded tools. They may seem expensive at the time but if you take care of your tools they will serve you well over the years.

Assess what you need to do the job and buy accordingly. Gradually build up your tools rather than go out and buy them all at once. This way you will value each tool more and take more time and thought in your selection.

Specialist modelling vices often look impressive but in

reality they lack strength and are inaccurate and expensive for what you get; it is far better to go for a good quality vice.

There is a wide range of good woodworking vices available, including machine vices which are specifically designed to be used in a drilling or milling machine.
Most metalworking vices can be fitted with smooth jaw inserts which will reduce the risk of marking work.

Knives are an important tool in the miniaturist's kit and the Swan Morton-type scalpel with size 10 or 10A bladesis particularly suitable for small work.

When changing a scalpel blade use a pair of pliers to remove the old blade.

A self sealing cutting mat is worth buying for light cutting and a safety rule with a recessed finger grip will help protect fingers.

For making small joints and cutting mitres, small razor saws and mitre guides as produced by Xacto are ideal.

Small, good quality, files, such as Swiss or needle files, are very useful but it is wise to make handles for them.

Watchmakers' screwdrivers make ideal miniature chisels. They are inexpensive and go down to a small size. Sharpen them regularly on an oilstone and strop.

A small square, such as an engineer's steel square, with a 75mm (3") blade is extremely useful.

Power Tools

Although most miniature work can be done perfectly well with hand tools, there comes a time when the miniature woodworker is likely to add power tools and machinery to his workshop. However, do not expect one machine to solve all problems!

Add a 12v miniature drill to your tool kit and you will wonder how you ever managed without one! A Minicraft or Proxxon drill, used with a transformer, is neater, more precise and safer than a full sized drill and such drills are capable of very high speeds. These tools are manoeuvrable and ideal for drilling in awkward places and can be used both freehand or in a drillstand. **FIG. 1** These drills can also be used for shaping, sanding, milling and routing with the appropriate accessories. The miniature router is also worth considering if you want to produce mouldings, grooves for inlay work and other small-scale routing work. When routing a high speed is required and a miniature 12v router, such as the Proxxon is a very versatile machine which can be used freehand in its plunge router mode or held in a drillstand for overhead routing.

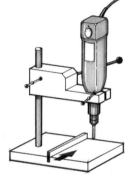

Overhead routing has an advantage because you can see clearly what is happening. (*Fig. 1*)

To produce mouldings for items such as picture rails, picture frames, dado rails, etc., pass the wood under the router several times using different cutters until you have achieved the required shape.

It is better to make a number of shallow cuts than to attempt one deep one.

It is important to feed the work without interruption or hesitation, otherwise the wood will burn leaving unsightly marks.

The miniature circular saw is an expensive machine and better results will be obtained with a machine such as the Proxxon mains saw than with a 12v saw, because the extra power is needed.

This machine is useful for cutting small strip wood or for cross-cutting sections of wood. With the aid of a mitre fence, angled cuts are simple.

Buy a supercut blade to achieve the best results; these are more expensive but give a smooth cut. The standard blade supplied with the machine is coarse and gives a rough cut.

Remember, these saws are only intended to cut thin wood (up to 9mm in the case of the Proxxon) and if you try to cut thicker wood you will stall the machine.

Use two small push-sticks when you are cutting very small sections of wood on a miniature circular saw. Remember, keep your fingers well away from the blade and keep the guard down. It might be a miniature saw but it can still give a very nasty unminiature-sized cut!

There are a number of small bandsaws which may be of interest to the miniature woodworker, in particular the three wheel Record, the two wheel Delta and the two wheel Proxxon.

Small pieces of wood can be dragged down by the blade through the throat plate so you can either temporarily hold them to a larger piece of scrap wood using an adhesive such as hot melt-glue or double-sided tape, or clamp a temporary table on the machine made up from a sheet of MDF with a very narrow hole cut for the blade to pass through.

The Powered Fretsaw

The powered fretsaw is a useful machine for the miniature woodworker when a number of intricate shapes need to be cut. The fine blades will give a very good finish with little sanding required. Buy the best machine you can afford and if you intend to do a lot of internal cutting seriously consider one of the Hegner machines with its brilliant patented method of blade changing.

Good lighting is essential. Natural light from a large window directly on to the work is probably the first choice.

FIG. 2

Polish the fretsaw table to make it very smooth so that friction is reduced and the work can move easily, but avoid using silicone based polishes because the silicon will be absorbed into the wood being cut inhibiting staining and varnishing at a later stage.

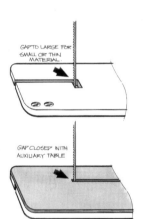

Mount the fretsaw on a rubber mat and bolt it firmly to a bench or table to reduce vibration. A temporary auxiliary table top made of ply or MDF can be made with a very fine hole through which the blade can pass. This can be clamped to the fretsaw table with double-sided tape and will enable very small pieces of work to be cut without the risk of them being dragged down through the throat. (*Fig. 2*)

The finer the blade, the finer the cut. Use the finest tooth blade you can for each particular cutting task. Hegner suggest No 2 blades to cut 0.5mm to 5mm wood, No 5 blades to cut 5mm to 30mm wood and No 9 blades to cut 30mm to 50mm wood. (*Fig. 3*)

FIG. 3

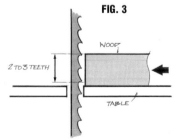

It is absolutely essential that the blade is put into the fretsaw so that it cuts on the down strokes and with very fine blade, this can pose a problem to those with less than perfect eyesight. A small magnifying glass is a useful addition to any workshop. If the blade is held against a white sheet of paper it is easier to see which way the blade tips are pointing.

If your fretsaw takes pin-ended blades you can grind off some of the pin each side of the blade so that the blade can be passed through a smaller hole for inside cutting. Fretsaw blades have a limited life so do replace them when they are blunt.

For very fine work the performance of a blade can be improved by rounding the back of the blade slightly with an oilstone whilst the machine is actually operating.

Fretsaw blades are stamped out during manufacture and therefore they usually have a slight burr on one side only. Again, a gentle touch with the oilstone when the machine is running can smooth this burr off to obtain a finer cut. (*Fig. 4*)

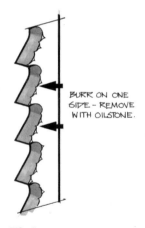

BURR ON ONE SIDE - REMOVE WITH OILSTONE.

FIG. 4

The experienced operator should have no difficulty in following a straight or curved line providing that he chooses a sharp blade, has a fine line to follow and has a good light to see the line. Nearly all fretsaws will tend to cut to one side by 1 degree or 5 degrees depending on the material being cut. This is one reason why a parallel fence is of little use on a fretsaw. If the blade does wander slightly when cutting a straight line, true the line up with a fine file or a small sandpaper block rather than trying to recut with the fretsaw.

If you are using a paper pattern or photocopy, this can be glued to the wood using low-tack spray glue or a rubber based cow gum.

Shade the waste areas grey, not black, so that you can see the blade clearly. Peel or sand off any remaining paper when the cutting is complete.

Practise on scrap material before attempting work on very complex patterns or on expensive exotic woods.

Cutting out shapes, such as a recess for a dolls' house window, is greatly improved by drilling very small holes in each of the corners.

A number of identical shapes can be cut out in one operation by making a sandwich of materials. The sandwich can be held together with double-sided tape, ordinary glue or with staples.

If double-sided tape is used, avoid actually cutting through the tape because it tends to clog the blade.

When cutting a sandwich of thin plywoods accept that the bottom layer will probably have some whiskering and might not be usable.

Machines with two speeds, or a range of variable speeds, do offer advantages. The speed can be reduced for very hard wood and, with very intricate work, a low speed can be selected to start the work; this will improve accuracy.

Miniature Turning

A wood-turning lathe will greatly increase the range of items a miniature woodworker can make. With practice and patience very tiny items can be produced such as ship's wheels, belaying pins, dead eyes, etc., for model ships and legs, feet, knobs etc., for miniature furniture. You need to choose your lathe with care. A lathe for miniature turning needs to be accurate and capable of high speeds of at least 3000 rpm and it needs standard

MT holes, preferably 1 MT, in the headstock and tailstock. A lathe which meets all these criteria is the Tyme Little Gem lathe which has a variable speed of 0-5000rpm; it is ideal for very small work and has the advantage of being portable, quiet and relatively easy to use.

Many turners carry out miniature work on a full size lathe, for example of a Harrison Graduate fitted with a 4-jaw self centring chuck. Clearly the skilful turner can produce excellent results, but a small lathe, such as the Little Gem or Carba-Tec, is much easier and safer to use for miniature work. Small metal turning lathes, such as the Unimat, are often used by modellers to good effect but sawdust in the leadscrews, etc., does tend to increase the risk of rusting. The turner needs uninhibited access to the work on the lathe to produce good flowing curves and the toolholders, etc., on a metal turning lathe tend to get in the way.

Keep the lathe clean and remove any polish, etc., which has fallen on the bed bars. The metal parts should be lightly rubbed with oil to prevent rust. Keep the MT holes clean and do not hammer pieces of wood on to the headstock drive; remember the bearings are relatively small. Keep the spindle headstock thread clean and avoid damaging it. Make sure the threaded holes on any accessories are kept clean. If you respect your machine and take good care of it you should have a useful and reliable lathe for a good many years.

A small drill chuck with a suitable MT shank is a very useful accessory for holding small items in the headstock. (*Fig. 5, next page*)

A small face plate can be used to make a glue chuck or a cup chuck and small screw chucks are useful. (*Fig. 6, next page*)

A revolving centre reduces the need to lubricate the end of a spindle at the tailstock end and is well worth the expense. (*Fig. 7*)

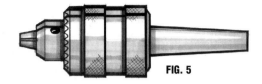

FIG. 5

The Multistar Micro Combination Chuck, although expensive, offers a wide selection of holding methods to the miniature turner. Moreover, the chuck body has 24 index holes enabling the turner to drill accurate holes at regular intervals, for example, at the rim of a wheel for spokes or to flute a chair leg. It is important that any chucking system used has no sharp edges or jaws sticking out and the Multistar meets this requirement fully. A small screw chuck is available as an extra.

THICKNESSED WOOD SCREWED TO FACE PLATE.

WOOD GLUED WITH SUPERGLUE, HOT MELT GLUE OR D/SIDED TAPE.

FIG. 6

Small turning tools, such as the range of Ashley Iles miniature turning tools in HSS steel, make life much easier for the miniature turner. The range is comprehensive and the most useful tools are: the small roughing out gouge; the skew chisel; and the small spindle gouge. With these three tools most spindle turning operations can be carried out. (*Fig. 8*)

A small scraper (*last item, Fig. 8*), which can be ground as required, will be useful for little bowls and boxes.

When choosing tools for very small work, such as 2mm (1/12") scale chair

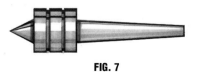

FIG. 7

FIG. 8

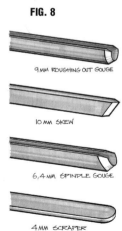

9 MM ROUGHING OUT GOUGE

10 MM SKEW

6,4 MM SPINDLE GOUGE

4 MM SCRAPER

legs, it is a mistake to select tools that are too small because they lack rigidity. The Ashley Iles 12mm oval (½") skew chisel is rigid but not too large to turn the most intricate beads.

FIG. 9

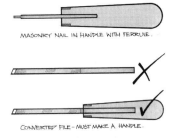

MASONRY NAIL IN HANDLE WITH FERRULE.

CONVERTED FILE - MUST MAKE A HANDLE.

Very small gouges can be difficult to use and one of 4mm (5/32") or more will be easier to control,

It is possible to make your own small chisels out of HSS or silver steel blanks but masonry nails are particularly useful since they can be ground relatively easily and yet they retain their hardness. They make very good scrapers and parting tools for turning items such as very small goblets. (*Fig. 9*)

Drilling in the lathe is usually carried out with the work held at the headstock end and the drill mounted in a drill chuck at the tailstock end. The work is rotated and the tailstock wound in to carry out the drilling.

It is important to make sure that the drill does not bind in the hole and that the shavings are removed by bringing the drill out from time to time.

FIG. 10

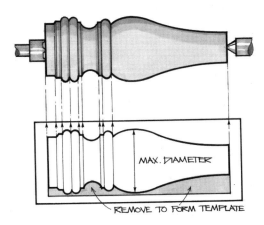

MAX. DIAMETER

REMOVE TO FORM TEMPLATE

It is essential that the headstock and tailstock are accurately in line or the drill will wobble and run out of true.

Always use sharp drills!

Repetitive turning demands planning and practice. Simple guides or templates can be made to aid the turner to develop the shape of a spindle in exactly the same way, say for four identical chair legs. (*Fig. 10, previous page*)

Use a pair of callipers to measure the diameter of the work regularly and the results should be satisfactory.

Make a few extra spindles and then you can select the best match!

The turner is spoilt for finishes that can be used on the work whilst still in the lathe. Coronet Speed-an-Eez friction polish will give a high gloss, instant finish. Oils such as Rustin's Danish Oil and Liberon's Finishing oil give a good satin finish with the advantages that additional coats can be applied to the work after assembly; these oils are safe, economical and easy to use.

FIG. 11

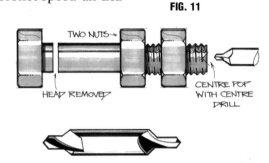

TWO NUTS→

HEAD REMOVED

CENTRE POP WITH CENTRE DRILL

The turner will often need simple jigs or mandrels to hold work in the lathe and a small bolt with the hexagon head removed can be utilised as a mandrel to turn one or several small wheels. The mandrel can be held in a drill chuck in the headstock end. (*Fig. 11*)

If several wheels are to be turned in one operation, it is wise to centre pop the outboard end of the mandrel so that it can be supported in a revolving centre in the tailstock end to give rigidity.

A very useful small drill for the model maker is a centre drill which can be used to form a centre pop on the outboard end of a home made mandrel.

Superglue can be used for an instant bond but make

sure that you are working in a well ventilated area as some superglues have strong smelling activators which some turners find unpleasant.

Another option is to use a hot-melt glue such as Esco 100 second. Such glues are odourless and instant but take care as hot glue can burn.

FIG. 12

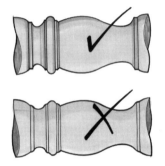

If expensive exotic woods are being turned it is worth gluing them to a scrap piece of wood which has been secured to a small face plate or screw chuck, thus avoiding wastage.

Offcuts of 19mm (¾") or 25mm (1") thick hard woods from your local joiner can be made into very good glue chucks and they may well be free!

For spindle work the turner should aim to use as little abrasive as possible, as sanding tends to round off the crisp corners that the turner is aiming to produce. Good results can be achieved by keeping the chisel sharp and by keeping the bevel close to the wood. (*Fig. 12*)

For small items, such as 1/12" spindles, the instant speed variation of the Little Gem is a distinct advantage since the speed can be stepped up as the diameter is reduced. The smaller the diameter the faster the speed is the general rule. The result will be a really fine finish. The lathe is so designed that a little spindle can be supported by a finger at the rear edge to reduce the risk of whipping but be warned, at 5000rpm all but the most hardened fingers will suffer!

Gluing

There is a bewildering selection of glues to choose

from, but the following are particularly recommended because they are low odour, have a solvent-free base, are free from harmful vapours and are therefore relatively safe to use.

PVA adhesive is an excellent woodworking glue.

For a waterproof and gap filling glue, Cascamite is a good choice. Dunlop Powerfix is a reliable and easy to use contact adhesive.

Araldite epoxy resin has many uses and is particularly good for securing small fittings such as tiny hinges; these can be glued on before pinning or screwing for a secure fix. The same method can be used to fix piano hinges on dolls' house doors. First screw the plane hinge into position and ascertain that the door hangs well and shuts correctly then remove the hinge and Araldite it into position before reinserting the screws. For very small items, superglues such as Dunlop SAS 2000 are invaluable. They give an instant bond but caution is needed when using them and they do have a limited shelf life.

Hot melt glue, such as Esco 100 second, is quick and is useful for glue chucking wood for turning and for holding small pieces temporarily to larger scrap pieces.

All these glues need to be stored and used at room temperatures to perform at their optimum best and cold, damp workshops should be avoided.

There are many ways to hold your work whilst the glue is setting. Inexpensive ways include strong rubber bands, clothes pegs, bulldog clips and masking tape.

A role of masking tape 19mm (¾") or 25mm (1") wide is a must in any modelling workshop. In addition to its primary role for masking areas to be painted it can be

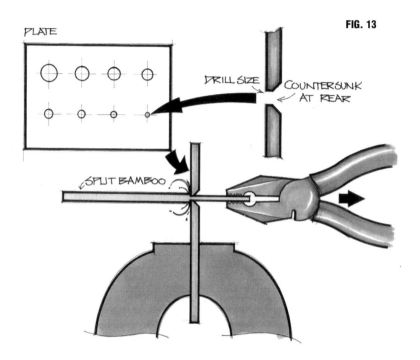

FIG. 13

PLATE

DRILL SIZE

COUNTERSUNK AT REAR

SPLIT BAMBOO

used for holding items together whilst glue dries, marking out dimensions on wood, labelling wood and holding carcasses temporarily together. Wrapped around a twist drill it will act as a temporary depth guide; it will hold veneer whilst it dries in position, hold sandwiches of wood for fretting and hold paper to a home made drawing board. The list is endless!

Dowelling

Small dowels of 3mm (⅛") diameter or less have many applications in miniature woodwork. A wood dowel will form an integral part of a wooden item – it cannot rust, it is unobtrusive and no filling is needed.

Bamboo is an excellent material for making small dowels; it is strong, durable and readily available.

To make your own accurate dowels you need a piece of steel plate about 2.5 to 3mm thick in which you drill holes of decreasing size; the holes should be countersunk on one side. The holes should range from 3mm diameter to, say, 1mm diameter. The bamboo is pulled through the hole with pliers, working down to the desired diameter. Do not try to remove too much bamboo at once. (*Fig. 13, previous page*)

To increase the grip on each strip of bamboo you can fold a piece of abrasive paper over the end, with the abrasive inside and grip the whole with pliers.

If you standardize on the size of dowel, for example 3mm and 1.5mm, you can prepare batches so that you have a stock handy plus the appropriate drill.

To use the dowel, drill the dowel hole with a 12v drill the same size as the dowel, slightly sharpen the end of the dowel, dip into PVA adhesive and hammer gently home. Pare off surplus dowel with a sharp chisel when the adhesive is dry.

Finishing

Making a small item can be a relatively straightforward and quick operation, but when it comes to finishing time and patience are needed! It is at this stage that many models are spoiled.

All saw marks, burrs and whiskers must be removed from the work and this is done with careful sanding. Start with 120 grit and work through to 600 grit to get a really good smooth, blemish-free, finish. A selection of aluminium oxide cloth-backed abrasive marketed under the name J Flex in 120, 240, 400 and 600 grits will be suitable for most uses. Because this type of abrasive is flexible it can get into awkward nooks and crannies and if it becomes clogged it can be washed out in warm soapy water and used again. J Flex can be bought by the metre in various widths.

Before applying any woodstain, wax, paint or varnish all dust and any grease must be removed from the surface of the wood and the work needs to be finished in a dust-free atmosphere allowing plenty of drying time between applications.

Products such as Rustin's Danish Oil and Liberon's Finishing Oil are easy to apply and give a good finish.

Kiwi light tan shoe polish gives an excellent wax finish!

Too many models are poorly finished in thick, runny, dark gloss varnish and hours of painstaking woodwork is ruined. Keep your finish thin and as realistic as possible. Sanding sealer, French polish or diluted polyurethane varnish are all suitable if used correctly. The secret is to use many thick coats, allowing plenty of drying time between them, rather than a few thick ones.

An airbrush is an option which should be considered by the serious modeller because it is possible to apply extremely thin coats of finish to an item.

Acrylic paints, varnishes and stains are now widely available in a range of colours. These products are safe, odourless, non-toxic and dry quickly. They have the great advantage that brushes can be washed out in water.

CARVING

What To Carve

Unless you have decided what to carve start looking at other work.

If you have decided, you should also start looking at other work. Museums and historic buildings are good for inspiring some ideas.

Specialist books and magazines are a good source of visual information and, importantly, written text to be followed. The woodworking press usually carries adverts for specialist publishers, or you could try libraries as your source.

Galleries, art shows and exhibitions are all a good source: watch local and national press for forthcoming events, etc.
If travelling to museums, etc., make sure that they have work in their collections and that it is presently on show to the public.

If you have local carvers/sculptors in your area, visit them. Make an appointment first.

More and more videos on carving are become available.

Join the British Wood Carvers' Association.

If you have a strong desire to carve a life-size replica of the Tower of London then get on with it, don't be put off by the others who say you can't. You can if you put your mind to it.

For most, perhaps something on a lesser scale will be
what's wanted but even something very small, say
something you could hold in your hand could be very
detailed and extremely difficult.
For those attempting carving for the first time, for many
reasons, such as lack of equipment, space, etc., go for
something like a bowl, globe or egg.

Don't confine yourself to one type of timber, do the
same exercise in different timbers and if necessary take
notes and photographs on how the timber works and
finishes. These "simple" exercises will show you how
the timber works, how to overcome holding difficulties,
how a finished form is reached, when to stop and how a
particular timber finishes.

This can all be held for future work when choosing a
type of timber for a particular project.

Working Equipment

Buy only the best and new equipment. On the whole it
will last longer, function better and have the benefit of a
guarantee.

If you like searching through second-hand tools then
some bargains can be had, but more than likely you will
be disappointed. Only an expert or years of costly
experience will provide you with good tools from this
source.

Personally handle and see the tools/equipment work
before buying. Practically, this is not always possible.
When buying by mail order, talk to the staff, they can be
very helpful and it is in their interest that you get the
right items.

Buy only from reputable dealers and get a catalogue.
This is helpful as the catalogue may contain tools that

you do not even know exist. Many descriptions of the tool and its particular uses may be included and you can be regularly updated with developments.

Workstands

There are many on the market. Most of them work so as to tilt the work in a variety of ways, speeding up and helping the modelling process with the work positioned atop and free of any clamps.

Most work on a large steel ball system being held mechanically or hydraulically, releasing the ball, moving the work, then retightening the ball.

Price will dictate the type bought, but remember, several hundred pounds' worth of workstand will be useless unless it is attached firmly to a completely stable bench.

How to Start a Project

After all your research and looking, collecting and making models, taking photos, etc., it will be common for a drawing to be produced (some works can be done freehand).

Drawings should ideally be of the same size as the finished project or to a suitable scale.

A squared grid scaled or to size is the most convenient way.

Don't ignore modern technology: computers with graphics programmes, scanners and printers are very handy and quick tools.

Three-dimensional work needs at least two sides drawn and would benefit from all four and other angled views.

Working in the round it is especially hard to convey perspective from drawings to the working blank. A model made from plastocine or clay is best for accuracy in details, sizes, etc. Make sure that the model is built on to an armature to support it if it is too large to support its own weight.

Relief work will also benefit from prior modelling.

An outside line plan will be needed for profiling either with a fret saw or bandsaw. It will be discovered when carving that details drawn on will disappear, so don't waste time with these. They should be drawn on at the relevant later stage of modelling.

When profiling a three-dimensional piece it will be necessary to include at least one other side, i.e: front and side. The timber section needs to be square and a centre line drawn on the two sides with top and bottom lines for alignment of the two drawings.

This profiling saves a lot of laborious chopping work and if accurately done gives you a place to start marking off, form and details, albeit a squared version of your carving. Putting it simply, you only have to round the corners off!

Use a router if possible on panel work to profile.

With a project as simple as the bowl, egg or globe shape a drawing is not strictly needed, but make one if you feel you need one as it is good practice.

A drawing needs to be transferred to the blank. This can be done freehand, traced using carbon paper or with a stencil.

Don't use a pen with very liquid ink, as this may get drawn into the fibres of the timber, not only distorting

the pattern, but marking areas to be saved.
A pencil is best, or a scribed mark, but think whether
this type of mark is acceptable in the finished work.

Having drawn on the outline the piece can be sawn. If
there is a difference in the drawing, cut the easiest
route first and save these waste pieces. The drawing
can then be replaced with pins (don't pin through the
carving) or taped back in place to cut the other side.

A bandsaw is not necessary for small work – a fret saw
or treadle saw will do. Doing it by hand though leaves
some room for inaccuracy. A helping guide would be to
drill a series of holes around the outside, but the drill
needs to be sent through square. A pillar/bench drill
would ensure accuracy.

On even smaller work it could be crosscut to the line,
then that waste chopped away with a gouge or chisel.

For large work then a chainsaw will be needed, and
more than you would think can be achieved with one of
these. However, they are beasts and should only be
used by people with the confidence, training and the
safety equipment that must go with them.

Cutters available for angle grinders will also prove
useful in waste removal and modelling. They are,
however, to the uninitiated quite frightening, and noisy
and messy too. Use safety clothing and follow the
makers instructions carefully.

Flexible shaft-drive machines and their cutters and
burrs are very useful for all manner of waste removal,
modelling and fine detailing. Don't bother with drill-
driven attachments of this type as they don't revolve
quickly enough.

The adze has been used for thousands of years for

waste removal and modelling. It's similar to an axe but the cutting head is arranged on the handle horizontally to the vertical. Axes generally are not suited for carving, except for the smaller side axes.

Working Practice When Working on a Project

PLAN AND MAKE NOTES

Plan how you are to work on a figure. Is it best to work on the whole or a section at a time? Picture the scenario; where you have worked a piece of a figure that for later work may need to be held risking soiling or damage. Or working a section that may need to support the whole at a later stage and finding it is not strong enough!

Also, don't forget to pre-plan for finishing and fixing; even the signature can sometimes be best done beforehand!

Generally, gradual waste removal is best. Don't hack off great lumps – there is a grave risk of taking too much. Continuous movement of the carving is the price to pay but this will aid the overview of what you are doing.

It is often said that you can take it off but you cannot put it back on. This is not strictly true as an arm for instance could be glued back into place, but it was more than likely bad planning and/or haste that knocked it off in the first place!

When clamping work in a vice or a G clamp, never overtighten the clamp. Place the work in the vice and progressively tighten, checking as you go by pushing or tapping with a mallet to see if the vice or clamp will hold the piece. If you don't do this you risk damage to the piece, equipment or yourself. Do not start work until you are satisfied that it is safe to do so.

Making Cuts

It is tempting to start your first piece with great gusto.
Think, slow down, take your time. The trick with all
sculpture involving removal of waste is to know when
to stop. If this stage is not reached with care then you
might rip out or split areas that you had been intending
to keep.

Holding a chisel or gouge, let us first distinguish the
difference in the two tools:
Chisels are flat, gouges are rounded.
However, there are many thousands of types, sizes and
shapes of carving tool available, although these can be
separated into three main types.

    a) Chisels, which have a straight cutting edge.
    b) Gouges, which have a rounded cutting edge.
    c) V tools, which have a V-section cutting edge.

All of these come in differing styles i.e: straight, (this
refers to the shank), swept, bent, back bent, forward
bent and cranked.

The shape of the shank can differ from round to square.

The cutting end can also be of differing styles, tapered,
straight or fishtail.

Most of these tools can also be purchased in a skew
form, which means that the cutting edge has been cut
off at an angle and are also available skewed left or
right.

You don't need all these tools to carve, just a few of the
more basic types will do for many types of carving. The
purchase of more specialist tools should only be
contemplated should a particular project require them.

All chisels and gouges are designed to be used with a handle. Most are wooden, some are plastic. These are fitted into the handle with a tang of metal formed from the end of the shank and are sometimes secured by a ferrule.

There are two types of handle: long or short, the latter usually being formed into a mushroomed shape to fit the palm. This is the type favoured by block cutters, etc., but is perfectly suitable for carving of all types.

The longer, straighter handles are more common as they can be pushed by hand or by the tap of a mallet.

Use a round-headed mallet for carving, not a joiners' square-headed mallet. As you are continually changing direction with the gouge the round head of the mallet will, more likely than not, contact with the end of the handle and there is more chance that the square-headed mallet will glance off the end of the gouge handle.

The longer handled chisel/gouge can be held and worked with one hand or two, holding either all the handle or partly holding the shank (the area of metal from the handle to the cutting end) and either pushing the tool's cutting edge through the timber or forcing it through with the aid of a mallet being tapped on the end of the handle as lightly or as hard as required.

When pushing the gouge by hand, two will be better than one: one pushing, the other controlling direction and depth.

Don't cut directly down into timber on the line you wish to keep: this will force timber fibres to break and these will then come away when you chop to this line.

Chase around the line with a V tool, then with the

chosen gouge cut waste away to the outside of the line.

Re-cut the line with the V tool to gain more depth.

When working three-dimensional pieces, wherever possible work away from the timber you wish to keep. This helps to avoid gouging out if you slip and also eases the final modelling, as the kept portion can be easily pared down to the desired size and shape.

Apart from not having sharp tools or the work not being held conveniently or firmly, messy work can be caused by not using the right tool for the job. For instance, when modelling a face, the eyes, nostrils and inside mouth can be shaped with a gouge that fits the drawn line exactly, but a straight gouge would not be ideal as the follow on from the rest of the tool shank can bruise and damage the shape/form desired. A fishtail shaped cutting edge would be far better, as the cutting edge is the widest part of the tool so that there is no real follow on problem with these types.

When modelling, sometimes you might feel that it is not turning out as you had hoped. Stop and think. Rather than a lack of ability it may well be the wrong tool type, shape, size or bevel that is the problem.

When rounding off an area don't be tempted to cut the corner flat, actually round it, pare down gently to the desired form.

Take small cuts at a time; you will be surprised how deep a well struck gouge can go!

When carving, if any resistance is felt in the timber stop and try to cut from another direction. If you push too far then you risk tearing out timber you wished you had not!

How to Finish

Chisel and gouge cuts have been the norm through the ages, but modern tools and abrasives have opened up the possibilities for finer finishes.

To finish a work finely with just a gouge will require a lot of patience and tact. Through experience it will become evident that not all timber will cut the way you want it to, especially against the grain. Check the sharpness of the edge, it may have dulled off. Only experience will tell you this has happened. Resharpen and have another gentle try, if unsuccessful then it might be time to turn to a file. Riffler files are the main type of files used in carving. These are variously shaped to find their way into awkward places.

Try the rotary burrs; at high speed and fine cutting grade they can be super for those difficult areas.

Don't ignore abrasive papers – these really are the most versatile method, if not so long-lasting. Abrasive paper can be torn, folded, screwed up and attached to other things to get that particular spot.

There are many types of paper. Basically, the rougher the paper to start the finer to finish. Be careful: some rougher papers can leave very deep scratches and only resorting to the gouge will clean these up.

Black emery-type paper can be disastrous on lighter coloured timber!

If sanding differing colours of timber that have been jointed together, keep the dust fluid with oil or white spirit. This stops the darker dust becoming embedded in the lighter. Wash down afterwards with white spirit.

A cabinet scraper (a tempered thin steel plate with a

fine burr) is good, but only on large surfaces. A chisel or flattish gouge can be used to the same effect.

There is always a way to work out a problem; if needs be adapt or alter a tool to do the job. Stand back for a while and think, use your imagination, but don't be tempted to alter/disregard safety equipment/guards, etc., on mechanical tools.

Finishing Timber

If possible, do the finishing away from the soiled workshop.

If not, then make sure the area is well lit, well ventilated, clean and warm enough to dry a particular type of finish.

Once a finish has been applied it might be some hours before the piece can be moved/handled. Pre-plan for this.

There are many differing finishes that can be applied to timber. Some of the more basic tried-and-tested types range from French polish to modern polyurethanes, cellulose and acrylic lacquers, to the humble, but very effective, bees-wax and oils, as well as paints, gilding, stains and bleaching.

There are several rudimentary steps needed in order to successfully apply a finish. The surface must be dry, clean and free from grease.

Try out finish on offcuts beforehand. This will tell you if this is what you want and give a guide as to how best to apply it.

WOODTURNING

Woodturning is an ancient craft with a history going back some 4000 years. It is thought most likely that it was the Egyptians who were responsible for its development. Early lathes were vertically oriented, powered by one man with a cord, while another applied the tools and fashioned the wood. Lathes have developed a tremendous amount over the years of course, as have the tools and accessories you need to work with them. We can now have variable speed power (from 1rpm through to what you desire), etc. All this development is very impressive, with much of it coming in the last 20 years or so, but it remains a fact that there are those who use the barest minimum of technology and still create some wonderful work. It is not the equipment but the skill of the turner that will forever be paramount. You can have the finest equipment in the world, but if you don't have the necessary skills you are unlikely to create worthwhile objects. Most of these skills can be learnt: it is all down to practice and putting a lot of time and effort in, as with most things.

For most of its history woodturning has been seen purely as a craft, and the turner himself a producer of things useful. Things to eat and drink from, components for furniture and buildings, products of all sorts for use in the home, toys and tools to play and work with – the list is endless when you think about it. Artistic qualities in turning for the most part have been of secondary importance, function being the primary objective. Now, however, there is a strong movement of turners world-wide who are elevating this once humble craft to an accepted art form. For most it will still remain a craft, where in a very short space of time, minutes quite often, it is possible to create something useful. It has been described as a craft that offers "instant gratification and satisfaction", but for many it must also be said that until the skills are learnt "total frustration" is more applicable!

Lathes

This is a mine field: there is a lot of junk out there! Unfortunately, the ideal lathe doesn't exist, offering everything you would like to have. But remember, you can make small work on the big lathes, but not big work on small ones.

In general, as in everything else, buy the best you can afford, but identify the type of work you feel you are most interested in producing, as some lathes are much better suited to certain aspects of turnery.

If spindle work is your forte, then a lathe that has got a decent length capacity, nothing less than 915mm (36") would be useful, with a minimum swing of 254mm (10") over the bed.

FIG. 1

Tool rests that allow you to give finger support to slender turnings from underneath and above are best, strong but with no fanned wide taper, and the fanned type are best for headstock turning. (*Fig. 1*)

If you do a lot of long turnings, a long rest with two vertical stems is what you require and, of course, two saddles. (*Fig. 2, over the page*)

Any tool rest over 380mm (15") long on a single stem is usually not very good, as there is a tendency for flexing to take place at their tips. A 25mm (1") diameter minimum stem is required on rests of this size. There

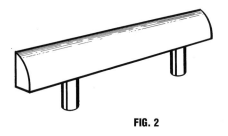

FIG. 2

are many made that are flimsy, weak and too flexible.

Avoid lathes that have spanner release for tool rest saddles and tailstocks: quick release handles and cam locks are what to look for.

Buy a lathe with a hollow spindle in both the headstock and tailstock, with a morse taper in each.

Many lathes are underpowered. 1/3hp and ½hp is common, which is fine for very small lathes and for small work, but I suggest ¾hp is the very minimum for a medium size lathe. 1hp and upward is what you really need, if you are serious about your turning. Below 1hp you can slow the lathe when taking heavy cuts, which is very frustrating. I am talking about single phase motors.

Most lathes sold in the UK are for bench mounting, if you purchase a lathe of this type build a solid base and secure the lathe firmly to it.

With headstock lathes I suggest a 406mm (16") diameter swing is the minimum requirement, with a spindle size of 32mm (1¼") being the minimum if headstock turning is your forte.

Good bearings are essential, and these should be well spaced on the spindle.

Toolrests should have a minimum 25mm (1") stem and be of the fan type for strength. They are best if when the top of the toolrest is positioned at centre height there is no more than 12mm (½") of the stem protruding from the saddle. This gives good support and limits any possibility of flexing. (*Fig. 3*)

Short bedded lathes are best for headstock work. They allow the user to use longer handled tools which make for more fluid application as they afford more leverage and control.

FIG. 3

Headstock lathes should be heavy, a single column casting is best, and if not of this type then they should be of the very heavy bench-mounted variety. These should be mounted on a good heavy gauge metal base, a concrete block, or a wooden boxed base made from plywood and timber and filled with sand.

Tools

High speed steel tools are a must. I am surprised the forged ones are still made, as the edge holding properties of HSS are so superior.

FIG. 4

There is a mass of tools to select from today, and some are for very specialized types of work. To start with at least, keep to the basics and build on these as your aspirations and skills increase.

Basic tool selection to get you started with spindle work: a roughing gouge, a spindle gouge, a skew chisel, a parting tool and a beading tool. I haven't suggested sizes as it depends on your work scale. (*Fig. 4*)

Basic tool selection to get you started with headstock turning: a bowl gouge, a domed scraper, and a straight scraper, again no sizes are given as it depends on work scale.
(*Fig. 5, over the page*)

HSS tools need to be sharpened on aluminium oxide wheels (usually white). These are softer than

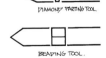

ROUGHING GOUGE.

SPINDLE GOUGE.

SKEW CHISEL.

OVAL SKEW CHISEL.

DIAMOND PARTING TOOL.

BEADING TOOL.

carborundum ones. Remember, the harder the steel the softer the grind stone. I use 60 grit aluminum oxide wheels and use my tools straight from the wheel, no slipstoning or honing.

FIG. 5

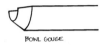

BOWL GOUGE

Chucking

This is an area of woodturning that has seen a surge of development in recent years. Most of the chucks are aimed at headstock turners. As with lathes, this area is a bit of a mine field. The better chucks expand and contract on a scroll mechanism like the engineering ones. The majority of these chucks are lighter than the engineers and operated with two levers. They all work, some better than others. I must say I don't much like levers (although I used this method for years); they are slow to use and unless you can lock your spindle you need three hands.

If you want a scroll chuck then the engineers' one with modified jaws for woodturners is the one to go for. It's more expensive but copes with any size of work and has a one-key operation.

Between centre work

I prefer a four prong dive centre as I feel this gives more grip and makes it more difficult to knock work off centre with heavy cuts.

A good quality revolving centre in the tailstock is best. My preference is for a ring centre rather than a cone one; penetration is less but the surface area is greater, thus spreading the weight more evenly.

Many of the imported dense hardwoods can split if you drive a prong centre into their end grain, so cut a cross about 2mm (1/16") deep in one end on the band saw for the prongs to locate in. (*Fig. 6*)

When turning thin spindle work there will always be whip. Most turners control this by supporting the spindle with the fingers of one hand. Either with an underhand or overhand grip, the thumb of the supporting hand is only in contact with the blade of the tool. (*Figs. 7 & 8*)

FIG. 6

Whip on thin spindles will be greater when using the heel of the skew, as there will always be a certain amount of forward pressure with the skew used in this way. Use of the skew with the point leading will minimise this a great deal. A straight across chisel is the compromise.

On difficult, wild, and short grained timbers the skew can often peck out small elements of this, giving a torn look. The use of a very modified spindle gouge with a long ground side angle drawn along the spindle with the bevel rubbing behind the cut usually solves this problem.

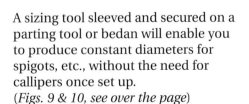

Never be afraid to modify tools, most of mine are not as the manufacturer supplied them.

FIG. 7

A sizing tool sleeved and secured on a parting tool or bedan will enable you to produce constant diameters for spigots, etc., without the need for callipers once set up.
(*Figs. 9 & 10, see over the page*)

FIG. 8

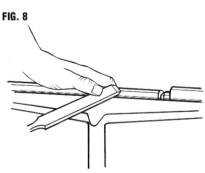

For repetitive size work such as spigots for chair rails, etc., I know turners who use sharpened open-ended spanners of the desired size to cut them.

FIG. 9

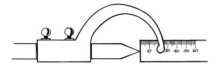

When turning bowls, etc., from cross grained timber there are two points where, when you are cutting directly opposed to the grain, they will often result in a rough or torn patch.

FIG. 10

Solutions

Great improvement can be obtained by softening the grain of this troublesome area with oil or soft paste wax and by taking light finishing cuts with sharp tools.

Use oil only if your product is going to be oil finished, oil waxed or finished, or shellac sealed and wax finished.

Use wax if you are going to use lacquer as a finish. Oil is not compatible.

Sheer scraping gives a cleaner cut on difficult woods. This means the scraper is tilted on its edge at an angle of usually 45% out of horizontal. Great care must be taken when this technique is used; the cutting must only take place in the lower section of the tool. The traditional way is safer, i.e., used flat on the rest with the cutting edge at centre height, the tool is tilted downwards 10-15% out of the horizontal. (*Fig 11*)

Spalted woods are very decorative but often have soft punky patches in them. Harden these with a cyanoacrylic glue such as super glue.

Prior to sanding timber that is spalted, seal with a lacquer and allow to dry. This will stop the black zone line dust from impregnating the lighter areas – making for a dirty looking piece.

Sand paper and garnet paper are not for woodturning: their cutting edge lasts a very short time. Silicone carbide and aluminium oxide abrasives are best.

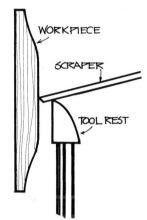

FIG. 11

WORKPIECE

SCRAPER

TOOL REST

I use wax or oil on my abrasives when I sand in the traditional hand-held way, depending on the product and finish to be applied. This method cuts down friction, heat and dust and gives a better finish. Abrasives like Wet & Dry, Trimite (silicon carbide) must be used and should be of the flexible type, i.e., softflex or superflex. If you fold a sheet and it cracks, you have the wrong sort.

I power sand most of my bowls with the soft rubber pads that have velcro-fixing matched sanding discs. I use a number of pads with the abrasive grits getting progressively finer. I mount these in a keyless chuck and only remove the abrasive disc when it is worn out. If you only have one pad and peel the discs on and off, you will find that the cloth on the back of the disc parts company before the abrasive. In the long term it pays to have more pads.

Final sanding is always carried out using hand-held very fine abrasives, with the lathe rotating, of course.

When polishing work with a natural top, edge, or with voids, always use paper towelling rather than cloth in case it catches. Paper will tear, cloth will grip. This way you will avoid damaging your work and yourself.

ROUTING & POWER TOOLS

FIG. 1

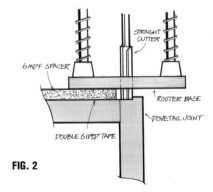

FIG. 2

When inserting cutters slightly withdraw them from the collet so that longitudinal vibration does not work the cutter loose.

Use masking tape on the router base to increase the friction and reduce it slipping for delicate freehand work.

When routing a rebate wider than the diameter of the cutter a quick and effective method is to set the fence to the full width of cut and first cut into the wood with the rotation of the cutter and then work across to the full width against rotation. (*Fig. 1*)

Trimming joints flush (e.g. dovetails) can be done easily by using a 6mm MDF spacer under the router with a cut out around the joints and setting a flat bottomed cutter to just touch the surface. Fix the spacer onto the workpiece with double sided tape. (*Fig. 2*)

Do not attempt to cut large grooves with a router as the more passes you make the more chance you will go off the line and the quicker the cutter will blunt. First mark out the groove and cut the walls 1mm inside the line and short of the depth with a portable circular. Then remove the waste with a chisel and mallet cleaving the grain and then trim the groove in one pass with a straight cutter. This minimizes the risk of the cutter wandering by making several passes and prolongs cutter life. In effect you are using the router as a precision trimming tool. (*Fig. 3*)

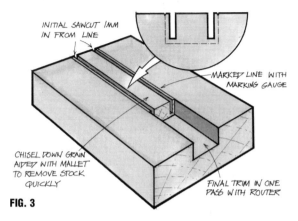

INITIAL SAWCUT 1MM IN FROM LINE

MARKED LINE WITH MARKING GAUGE

CHISEL DOWN GRAIN AIDED WITH MALLET TO REMOVE STOCK QUICKLY

FINAL TRIM IN ONE PASS WITH ROUTER

FIG. 3

When routing grooves and rebates make passes up and down the groove to remove feathered edges.

Do not overtighten when inserting cutters. Try to align the spanner and use your hand as a vice. (*Fig 4*)

FIG. 4

When routing stand with legs apart, one foot slightly in front of the other. Hold the router with arms stretched so that you are leaning down and can see the cutter and work backwards or forwards for maximum control. Never work sideways. The movement comes from your body and legs, as the arms, particularly the wrist, are locked.

A general rule is to plunge to a depth which is no more than half the diameter of the cutter in any one pass.

FIG. 5

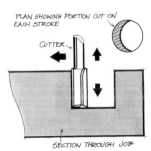

PLAN SHOWING PORTION CUT ON EACH STROKE

CUTTER

SECTION THROUGH JOB

The quickest way to remove stock (e.g. mortises) with a straight cutter is to execute a "rhythm" of fast plunge cuts, slightly overlapping the previous cut to a fixed depth. As the plunge action withdraws at the top of the stroke the router is moved in to cut the next overlapping cut. This is much quicker and more efficient than cutting a series of horizontal stepped passes. The reason is because you are breaking up short grain which means less fibre resistance and the chip clearance is fast because the overlapping cut represents less than half of the full diameter of the cutter. (*Fig. 5 previous page*)

When using the router for drilling holes or when starting the first plunge cut when mortising, it is important to ensure good chipping clearance either by using a spiral design cutter or by pre-drilling with a conventional power drill. A normal straight cutter will trap chippings, generate heat and result in burning wood and a dulled cutter edge if you do not take this precaution.

FIG. 6

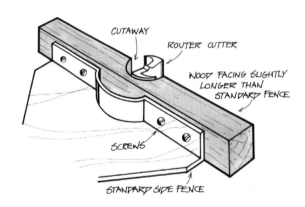

CUTAWAY

ROUTER CUTTER

WOOD FACING SLIGHTLY LONGER THAN STANDARD FENCE

SCREWS

STANDARD SIDE FENCE

To prolong the life of your router and expensive cutters, listen to the router motor. If the revs drop significantly you are overworking it and if smoke or burn marks appear you are either cutting too deep or the cutter is blunt. Cutters need to be razor-sharp with no resin build up, as this tiny piece of metal rotating at such a high speed (up to 27,000rpm), very quickly deteriorates if you do not treat it carefully.

A problem when using the straight fence is the router slipping at the beginning and end of the pass. Try screwing a wood fence facing onto the fence (*Fig. 6, previous page*), then carefully upturn the router and with fencebar screws lightly engaged, switch the router on and carefully push the wood facing into the cutter, withdraw fractionally, and then switch off. The fence support will now go right up to the shape of the cutter without actually touching it.

FIG. 7

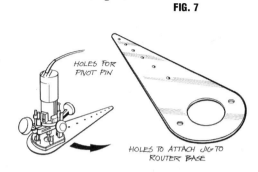

HOLES FOR PIVOT PIN

HOLES TO ATTACH JIG TO ROUTER BASE

When counterboring screw or bolt heads, try using a router for a cleaner and more precise cut. The recess can be routed out with a straight cutter after the shank hole has been conventionally drilled by careful alignment of the rotating cutter hovering just above the drilled hole.

When routing inside rebates on picture frames, etc., after the frame has been glued up, a 45 degree facing to the router fence can be used so that the router can cut up to the corner from one side and then away into the other side. You need a router such as an Elu 96 with long fence bars to achieve this.

There are numerous ways to cut large radii with the router. One of the simplest jigs is a sheet of 3mm (⅛") clear acrylic tapered from its attachment to the router base to a series of holes at the other end, allowing a pin to be attached to the wood at the desired radius. (*Fig. 7*)

Toggle clamps (of various sizes) are very useful for quickly securing routers to shop-made routing tables and for securing work in jigs. (Available from Planet Engineering & Trend Cutting Tools).

When freehand routing, lettering or other fine cutter shallow-depth grooving, with a little practice it is much easier to tilt the router at the end of the cut to "raise" the cutter than release the plunge at the risk of losing a precise line. This also applies to starting the cut.

Power Tools

FIG. 8

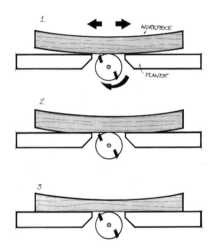

A common problem when using a fence on the bandsaw is for the saw to cut out of true, especially on thick pieces of wood. Almost as quick as using a fence with guaranteed accuracy is to mark a line (use a marking gauge for narrow cuts) and cut freehand to the line.

The bandsaw is remarkably useful for cutting internal shapes. The finer the blade teeth, the more control.

Use a timer switch when charging cordless batteries if it is inconvenient to be at hand when the charge is completed.

A mini cordless grinder is ideal for touching up chisels.

When tightening up a keyed drill chuck tighten all three positions in turn to ensure maximum and even grip.

When machine planing long pieces which are bowed, skate the convex side forwards and backwards across the cutter block from the centre in progressively longer strokes to take out the bow. Then execute entire passages as normal. The conventional method is to apply the concave surface to the cutter block but this can be too abrupt on the initial cut. (*Fig. 8*)

Always prepare the longest pieces to size first.

You can surface skim an irregular piece of wood by using the radial arm saw – raise the head so that the blade just "kisses" the wood and draw it across and as you move the blade back move the work simultaneously sideways for the next overlapping cut.

If you want to make a lattice work of halving joints quickly and accurately, use masking tape to bind the identical lengths together, mark out the thickness and spacing of the joints, set the radial arm saw to half the thickness and remove the slots. Take the tape off and reverse each alternative piece and fit the lattice together. (*Fig. 9*)

FIG. 9

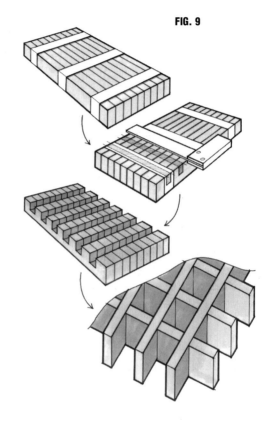

You can prolong the life of a jigsaw blade by placing a false platform under the sole of the jigsaw (e.g. 3mm (⅛") MDF. This causes a fresh portion of the teeth to be used but this method is best limited to thin work as on thicker work it might put strain on the reciprocating mechanism if you use a lower portion of the blade.

When using a bandsaw set up with a narrow blade for fine work, a false platform such as 6mm (¼") MDF can be fed into the blade and G clamped down ensuring total fibre support around the mouth of the blade.

FINISHING, PROTECTING & PRESERVING

In many uses wood needs to be protected, against wear, dirt or decay; in most "superior" uses its natural beauty is enhanced by finishing.

Here are some tips that will help you decide what type of finish is best for you, and help you get the best out of it.

WHY FINISH?
Wood is finished to give it an attractive appearance, and to resist, dirt, damage, wear, and, if used outdoors, weather.

FINISHES CAN BE USED FOR OTHER REASONS:
   to enhance features or hide defects;
   to emphasise variations or increase evenness;
   to make new wood look old, or old wood look new;
   to make cheap wood look expensive.
Decide what you want and choose your finish accordingly.

WHAT TO LOOK FOR IN A FINISH
The important features are: appearance, colour, lustre or sheen (gloss/matt etc); wear, scratch resistance; light fastness; ease of use. Relate to use; resistance to heat, water, alcohol for tables; to wear for floors; to weather for outdoors.
Choose a product that is fit for your purpose.

WHY PRESERVE?

Wood can be attacked by fungi; in some uses attack means decay, in others disfigurement.

Make sure that you get a product that gives the protection that you need.

SELECTING YOUR WOOD

Think of the finished appearance at the beginning: are you going to use softwood or hardwood? Do you want the wood to retain its natural appearance and features? Are you going to stain it to look like something different? Do you want knots or not?

When buying wood do not hesitate to sort it out.

If a piece has got more knots than you want, reject it. With soft woods you may have to compromise, but you should be able to get near knot-free runs of hardwood.

Reject warped or twisted wood.
Reject stained and discoloured wood.
Blue stain goes right through, and cannot be removed.
(Although you may want it as a feature.)
Yellow stains might indicate that wood will stain unevenly.
Reject very resinous pieces, or those with resin pockets.
Sapwood always takes up more dye and will stain darker than heartwood; does that matter?
Select pieces that match – it is easier than trying to hide differences with stains.

PREPARING

Screw holes and similar will be less obtrusive plugged than filled; align plug gain with piece.

SANDING

Sand with the grain.

For painting: use coarse sandpaper to remove paint or other thick coatings: then rub down with 100 grit (fine, F2) or 150 grit (1).

For dyeing, polishing or varnishing, start sanding planed wood with 100 grit (fine, F2) or 150 grit (1); finish with 240 grit (flour, 00) or finer.

When progressively using finer sandpaper, make sure that you have removed all score marks left by the previous (coarser) paper before going on to finer.

Do not use sanders, like drill-attached discs, that score across the grain when preparing for varnish or polish.

Pay particular attention to end grain and around knots.

If you intend to use a water based dye or varnish, after initial sanding, wet surface with water, re-sand when dry, and for finest work repeat.

Do not use a wire brush or wire wool on outdoor wood, or on oak or chestnut; any bits left on will rust and stain.

Remove wax from old furniture, floors etc., before refinishing; they reduce key, dull gloss finishes and may stop drying. Go over with wire wool and white spirit, wipe spirit off frequently, and apply more. Use 00 or 0000 wool on furniture, 0 or coarser on floors.

Use great caution with chemical, or hot air strippers on veneer; they may damage the glue, raise blisters, warp or split the veneer.

Dyeing And Staining

GET THE RIGHT STAIN
Scratch and wear resistance of colour; with dyes, the

underlying wood colour shows when the scratch is deeper that the stain or when the stained wood has worn away. Use deep penetrating dyes, best are solvent dyes, alcohol dyes penetrate less and are less scratch resistant, while water based dyes are least resistant. With coloured varnishes and stains based on pigments the colour is on the surface, wood shows through as the surface wears away. Do not use in situations of high wear.

Penetrating dyes include Colron and Cuprinol wood dyes.

Light fastness: products containing pigments have greatest light fastness. For dyes, water based dyes are generally fastest, alcohol fair, and solvent least, but all are satisfactory for indoor use.

Weather resistant: only some solid pigments are weather fast. Ensure that the product is specifically recommended for outdoor use.

Drying time: alcohol dries very quickly, water only slowly and solvent dyes intermediate.

WOOD DYE OR COLOURED VARNISH?
Wood dyes penetrate into the wood, although for a complete finish a clear varnish or polish must be put on top. As a generality, this system gives the best finish, especially in depth of colour, clarity of grain, and scratch resistance.

With coloured varnishes the colour is in the varnish. They offer the convenience that a complete finish can be obtained with one product. They require coats (no dye coat), and are more tolerant of unevenness in the wood or in preparation.

Test dyes and stains before using; colours vary on

different woods. Coat test piece with varnish or polish; colours show differently under finish. Chemical stains: ammonia, potassium permanganate, potassium dichromate, are only suitable for use on some woods.

GET AN EVEN STAIN
Put dye on liberally, allow to soak in, then wipe excess off. Find out whether your work will take dyes evenly. Uniformity and depth of colour depend on the natural absorption of the wood. Check before applying dye; wipe over with white spirit. Patchy take up, shown by shading, indicates that the dye will take unevenly. Areas absorbing most show darkest. Look for sapwood absorbing more than heartwood, for areas in the sapwood that absorb even larger amounts (due to bacterial infection), around joints and on plywood where take up may be reduced by glue. Look for irregular grain and effects of poor preparation. Allow the white spirit to dry before continuing with dye or varnish.

For important work, test twice, before you do anything else. Firstly, to check the wood, and again immediately before staining, to check for glue and correct preparation.

If it looks as though your wood is going to take a dye unevenly, use a coloured varnish; these do not penetrate so much and so are less affected by any unevenness in the wood. If variations in your wood are great, seal with a thin coat of clear varnish, then use the coloured varnish. Do not put dye on after a seal or varnish. It won't work properly.

Varnishing and Polishing

GET THE RIGHT VARNISH OR POLISH
Wear, scratch and knock resistant: best, polyurethane, some water based acrylics; poor, French polish; worst,

waxes.
Ease of renewal: wax can simply be put on again, all
others need preparation before reapplication.
Resistance to heat, spills of water, or alcohol: best,
polyurethanes; worst, French polish.
Make sure you get an exterior varnish, or yacht varnish
for outdoor use .

POLYURETHANE VARNISHES
PU varnishes are the hardest wearing and most
versatile of modern finishes. There are many
proprietary makes, most offering several grades, thin
seals, brushing varnishes, in matt, satin or gloss, clear
or coloured. Many are bodied for brush application,
this for rag application, for thin coats, or to use as seals.

WATER BASED VARNISHES
Water based acrylic or polyurethane varnishes are easy
to apply, dry quickly, have little or no smell, and are
hard wearing. They cause grain raising and their gloss is
less than a good solvent polyurethane or French polish.

FRENCH POLISH
A good French polish is the most widely admired finish,
but needs the most skill in application; when finished it
is easily spoiled by water and alcoholic drinks. (Many
years ago, proof spirit was used to dissolve shellac to
make French polish...)

WAX POLISHING
Wax polishes are easy to apply and renew, but they are
easily spoilt by repeated handling, water or drinks.

Wax polishes need many coats and much rubbing to
get a good finish; give a sealing coat of thin varnish first
and you will get a good polish sooner. Use French
polish or a polyurethane varnish; thin polyurethane
with about 10-20% white spirit.

GET A GOOD FINISH

For a quick job: choose a thickish varnish with good "body", and brush on; only brush out enough to avoid runs and curtaining.

For a good job, build up with several thin coats.

Do not varnish in a dusty place; on a nice day, outside may be better than in your workshop.

Thin the first coat of oil based varnishes with 10% white spirit. It penetrates better and gives a better key.

Thin the last coat of oil based varnishes with 10-20% white spirit, and apply with a rag. It goes on more evenly, avoids brush marks, and air bubbles collapse more easily.

Rub down between coats: it improves adhesion between coats and removes dust specks, brush marks and any unevenness.

Hard varnishes, like polyurethane, can be cut back fast and fine with wet and dry carborundum paper. Wet paper with water, but not enough to soak into wood.

Use rags that are lint free and absorptive: cotton is best; silk, wool, nylon, polyester, acrylics and most synthetics are unsuitable. For French polish, make a "rubber" by wrapping lint free cloth around cotton wool.

VARNISHING VENEER

When finishing veneer stuck on with a contact adhesive (Thixofix or Evo-stick impact adhesive), or ironed on using glue sheet, or a preglued iron-on veneer, be aware that the solvent in many wood dyes and varnishes will soften the glue and may loosen the bulge. Best to build up a finish with several very thin coats, rubbed on with a rag. Do not thin the first coat, even though this might be recommended for other work.

French polish does not affect these glues; nor do water based stains and varnishes, but they may cause swelling of the veneer. Water based products need more rubbing down because of grain raising. Be careful not to go through thin veneers.

Finish salad bowls with salad oil (olive oil, sunflower oil or any polyunsaturated cooking oil).

FINISHING TEAK
Teak is a problem wood to finish. Natural oils interfere with drying of varnishes and dull polishes and the open grain makes getting a flat, glass-like surface difficult.

The best finish is a proprietary teak oil. Use a heavy one like Cuprinol Teak Oil for garden furniture and a light one such as Colron Teak Oil for reviving indoor furniture.

A simple, one-time amateur favourite finish is petroleum jelly (vaseline). Apply sparingly, as too much leaves the wood greasy.

If you want to finish with a gloss polyurethane varnish, then first wash the teak with a rag wetted with white spirit and wipe dry (wear plastic gloves). Allow to dry. For a first coat, thin varnish with about 10% white spirit and apply thinly. Drying is likely to take three or four times longer than usual. Wait until dry then continue applying thin coats until you have the finish you want. Rub down between coats with wire wool and white spirit, wiping off each time. Drying, while slow, will improve with each coat. You may need 6 or more coats to get a good gloss.

If you want a really smooth finish you need a grain filler. Try out on a spare bit of wood – fillers, on teak, can be disappointing, you may prefer a bit of grain.

Exterior Stains

The advantages of exterior wood stains are that they do not seal water in like a paint, so there is less risk of decay (you still need a full preservative where there is a great risk of decay), they are easier to apply and are less likely to flake. Restaining is simpler and there is usually no need to clean extensively, although they do not last quite as long as paints – typically, three to five years against five to seven. In the very long term, 20 years or so, build up of dirt may be enough for it to need stripping back to bare wood.

Fix glass with beads when intending to use an exterior stain.

FINISHING FRONT DOORS
Even good clear varnishes (three coats) may last only about two years if exposed to the weather, particularly if exposed to full sunlight. A longer lasting finish can be obtained by using an exterior wood stain, which are protected from damage by sunlight. They give colour, but do not hide the wood. There is a wide range to choose from; some are better on hardwoods, some on softwoods. Those made for hardwoods generally look best on doors.

Painting

HOW MANY COATS?
For new wood, primer, followed by undercoat and then topcoat.
Use primer specifically intended for wood.
For hardwoods, resinous softwoods, or to seal in stains: use aluminium undercoat. Check the label to ensure that it is suitable. (Use two priming coats if stain shows through first coat.)

If primed wood is left outdoors, without being fully finished, for more than four months (two months if water based), apply a second coat of primer.

For repainting wood: primer on bare patches, followed by undercoat, then topcoat.

Some painters prefer four coats:

Two undercoats if needed to hide previous colours, or to increase build.

Two topcoats, to develop colour more fully or to improve gloss.

Traditional painters preferred an intermediate coat (after undercoat and before topcoat) of a mixture (1:1) undercoat and topcoat. This gives a more gradual change from undercoat characteristics to topcoat.

Preserving

PREVENT DECAY, GET THE RIGHT PRESERVATIVE
True wood preservatives prevent decay of wood, whereas other products protect wood against weather and fungal staining, but not against decay. It is possible to be misled.

True wood preservatives protect against decay, wet and/or dry rot. Examples are creosote and Cuprinol wood preservers.

Exterior wood stains mostly contain a fungicide to protect against fungi that grow on a disfigured wood, but they do not protect against decay. Examples are Sadolins PX65, Cuprinol Wood Stains, Dulux Weathershield exterior wood stain.

Low priced water based Fence colours may contain

some fungicide to stop staining fungi developing until new fences, often made made with unseasoned wood, have fully seasoned. They will kill mould present when retreating, but offer only very short term protection against moulds and none at all against decay. Never use to protect fence posts. There are several makes, under names like Timbercare, Fencecoat or Fencelife.

When and how to preserve wood

WOOD DECAYS WHEN IT GETS WET, BUT NOT IF KEPT DRY

Wood in the ground or in touch with soil, manure or compost will decay in a few years unless protected. Consider preservation essential; get as much preservative as you can into the wood, preferably soaking for 2 or more hours. Manufacturers' instructions make specific recommendations for their product. Other outdoor wood may well rot and preserving is well worthwhile. A short dip or several brush coats is adequate. Furniture and articles that are only used indoors, including in sheds and the like, do not need preserving.

Structural timbers in buildings do not normally need preserving. However, there are a few exceptions for parts that are exposed on the outside: window frames, doors and frames, wood exposed at the eaves. (Window frames should be treated with a full wood preservative before paint or exterior wood stain finish is applied).

Which preservative?

Water borne preservatives can only be applied effectively by industrial processes. You can buy timber treated by pressure, this will give the longest life. It is worth buying fence posts, and fencing which has already been treated. They are available from most timber merchants and agricultural merchants.

Creosote is moderately cheap, and very effective, but it has a strong smell, and the wood remains oily and can stain clothes, hands, etc. Use on fences and outdoor wood. Do not use indoors, or on anything that is to be painted.

Organic solvent preservatives are the best choice for non-industrial use. They are very effective, can be applied by simple means, are clean, do not cause swelling and dry quickly. The treated wood is odourless and can be painted, stained, varnished or polished. (Check individual product labels).

SAFETY HINTS, TIPS & REMINDERS

Lifting and Handling

Before you start to lift and move a load, make these eight checks:

Is anybody or anything going to get in your way? Can the job be safely put down without trapping fingers?

Are you suitably dressed for the job? Make sure that you will not be hindered by clothing. Women should wear trousers or a divided skirt – a wide skirt could catch on the object as it is lifted. For safe carrying, loads need to be held close against the body. Worries about spoiling clothing should not stop you handling the load properly. See that nothing in your pockets will harm you, or the load.

Can you manage it? Test the weight of the load by trying to lift one corner. If you think it likely to be too heavy, get help or abandon the attempt.

Fig. 1

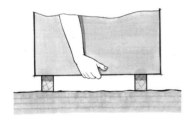

Will you be able to see where you are going? Check that you will be able to see over the load without straining.

Is the packaging secure? Will it remain intact while being carried?

Will the job harm you? Check for splinters and sharp edges.

Can the load be gripped properly? Get some packing underneath. (*Fig. 1*)

Is the load on safe ground? Check the safety of your footing.

Before you go, prepare the dumping site. To enable the load to be put down safely, install battens where necessary.

On your return to the pick-up site, re-check the route for obstructions and unsafe footing.

Using your spine as a crane jib is just asking for trouble. (*Fig. 2*). Do it this way.

FIG. 2

Get as close as possible to the load.

Make sure your hands are dry. Use suitable gloves when appropriate.

Grip with both hands at the same level.

Grip with your palms and roots of the fingers underneath the object. This should avoid stressing the fingers. Press inwards with the ball of your thumb. (*Fig. 1*)

FIG. 3

Set your feet about a hip's width apart, certainly not too widely spread or you might provoke a hernia. (*Fig. 3*)

If you will have to change direction as you lift, try to place your feet in a suitable position to avoid twisting your body.

Straighten, but do not stiffen, your back.

Tuck your elbows as close as possible against your sides.

Tuck your chin in.

FIG. 4

Take a deep breath.

Lift by straightening your legs, checking your balance as you go.

Balance your body to act as a counterweight while on the move. (*Fig. 4*)

Fire

If you must smoke in a workshop, create several safe parking sites, and never rest cigarettes, etc., anywhere else.

Keep a lid on the waste bin.

Rags impregnated with oils, solvents,waxes,etc., may

catch fire spontaneously. Keep them in metal fireproof containers having close fitting, preferably self-closing, lids.

Handle flammable liquids well away from open flames or running electric motors. Remember that some heavier-than-air fumes can run along the floor, under ducting or into inspection pits.
Make sure LPG (Liquid Petroleum Gas) cartridges are empty before detaching from the burner. Ejected fluid creates not only a risk of fire, but a risk of frostbite, for example to the eyes.

Chemicals and Dusts

Painful split skin at the ends of thumbs or fingers can be caused by chemical or dusty irritants. If you are a sufferer, try wearing finger stalls made from fingers/thumbs cut from rubber gloves.

Protect the skin from paraffin, turpentine, petroleum products, and strong solvent cleaners. They dissolve natural grease from the skin and leave it open to damage by other substances. Do not use solvents for cleaning your hands.

Always label your containers so that even after a period of time you will be able to know what they contain. Never, ever, mix solutions in a drinking vessel.
Keep your favourite beverage free from wood dust and shavings (or worse) by making a cover for your mug. The one illustrated overleaf is made by cutting the end from a plastic bottle. Make a slot in the side for the handle. (*Fig. 5*)

FIG. 5

Make a habit of extracting powders with a scoop or spatula. Shaking from containers produces dust which might be harmful. Powder could also float onto a job and maybe spoil it and all your hard effort.

General

Do not work with tools or machines if you are feeling upset, in a bad temper, or under the influence of alcohol or some drugs. Have a good tidy up instead, but avoid climbing or handling heavy objects.

Ordinary spectacles do not make good eye protection. When hit by something, they can smash into fragments which can damage the eyes.

Smooth the arrises of brand new chisels, or they may cut you. Avoid cheap hammers. Good quality hammers are "rim tempered", meaning that the head is less likely to chip. Flying fragments from the corner between the face and rim of the head can be dangerous to eyes, for example.

When working on electrical circuits, keep the mains fuse in your pocket. When appropriate, put a notice on the fuse box saying "Working on (such and such) circuit", just in case someone takes a fuse from elsewhere and renders your circuit live.

FIG. 6

Pick up small offcuts from the floor. Even a small one under a heel can cause a nasty fall. (*Fig. 6*) Pull out projecting nails when scrapping materials.
Use a chain to restrain vertically stacked boards so they will not fall and injure someone.

Remember the danger of trips from extension leads as well as the electrical hazards.

Always use a bench brush to sweep shavings from a bench or machine table. Your hand could catch on sharp hand tools or much worse.

Turning

Strips of abrasives, made from old cloth sanding belts, for example, can suddenly wrap round spindle work and take your hands with them. One consequence might be a broken wrist.

Machinery

Put a sticky label on your plug tops so that you know what is being switched on/off.

Always disconnect a machine from the electrical supply before making major adjustments. Use the isolator or pull out the plug. "No Volt Release" switches are magnetically operated. Machines controlled by them will not switch on when plugged in, nor will they re-start a machine after a power interruption. Some will automatically switch off if over-loaded.
If a job requires that two people have to cooperate on a machine (e.g., a drilling machine), agree who shall have sole control of the switch.

Do not hold anything in your hands (rulers, callipers, spanners, etc.) while operating the controls of a machine, or feeding a workpiece on a machine.

Keep a paintbrush in a suitable pocket. Use it for sweeping dust and swarf from around cutters. Never use a brush with a looped wire handle. Such brushes have been known to be caught by a rotating cutter and the loop has carried a hand or finger with them.

Rotating spindles can generate "windage", which can pull loose clothing, cuffs, ties, hair, bandages, string or handkerchiefs dangling out of pockets, etc., onto the shaft. After one revolution they can become firmly tied to the shaft and the worker is dragged onto the machine.

Bench Grinders

Adjust the tool rest as close to a grinding wheel as possible, certainly no more than 3mm (⅛"). The wheel could burst explosively if something jams between the rest and the wheel.

While grinding on a high-speed grinder the work can get hot. Do not hold work in cloth rags, or your apron.

Circular Saws

Each and every time there is a change in the size of the timber being cut, firmly discipline yourself to stop the saw and re-adjust the front edge of the crown guard to within half an inch (or less) from the surface of the wood.

Some riving knives have slotted ends fixed by two bolts to the saw's frame. When the riving knife is removed, for grooving or rebating, for example, the bolts must be tightened down so that they do not drift onto the saw blade. To save time and trouble in running down and tightening the nuts, make a dummy riving knife base like the one illustrated. (*Fig. 7*)

Make a "taking-off-table" or a roller to receive long material once it extends beyond the sawbench. Its rear edge should be located to keep helpers' hands at least 1.2m (4') from the up-running teeth of the saw. Unless you are short of space, a flat top is more useful than a roller.

FIG. 7

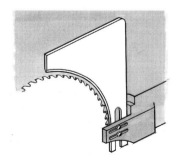

Controlling material at the end of a cut is easier if the fence of a circular saw does not guide the wood further than 50mm (2") beyond the tips of the teeth. Add suitable false fences to

FIG. 8

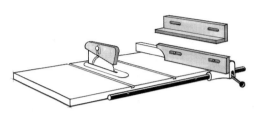

benches with long fences (useful for grooving and rebating). The "L" shaped attachment is helpful when the crown guard is near the fence, when cutting narrow strips, for example. It might well serve as your standard fence for most jobs. (*Fig. 8*)

Either of these false fences will prevent the potentially dangerous situation which arises when small offcuts can be caught by the upwards-running teeth. They can jam between the saw and the fence. The saw blade deflects and forcibly ejects the offcut forwards and upwards towards the operator, maybe hitting his/her face.

If you take a bit of extra trouble in making a posh push-stick you are more likely to use it, rather than take a risk by using any old offcut. Avoid fitting a loop of string, it might get caught in something at a critical moment. Push-sticks have been known to break and cause an accident. One made from a good quality plywood will be better. (*Fig. 9*)

Push blocks make small jobs easier and safer to handle. Use them with a push-stick in the right hand.
(*Figs. 10 & 11, see opposite page*)

FIG. 9

Beware of using wood-milling cutters in drilling machines. The chuck will be held in place only by the friction of an accurately machined taper. The sideways vibration generated when milling can cause it to come adrift, perhaps disastrously. (Engineers' vertical milling machines use a different taper which is held in place with a threaded "draw bar"

passing down the length of the spindle). Milling on a drill stand to which a power drill is fitted should not carry this risk since these chucks are screwed in place.

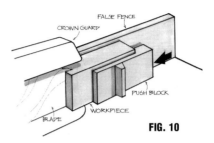

FIG. 10

The posture needed to get a good look at the point of a rotating drill can create a risk of scalping by getting hair entangled. Long hair is best secured behind the head with an elastic band or short ribbon.

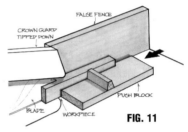

A key left in a chuck can fly out if the machine is started.

FIG. 11

As a drill breaks through the far side of a job, it can grab the work and set it spinning dangerously. Thin workpieces are difficult to hold safely. Try this holding device. (*Fig. 12*)

Routing and Power Tools

Power drills can jam, especially when the drill is breaking through. This can lead to a sprained hand or broken wrist.

FIG. 12

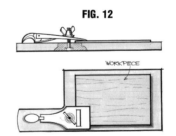

Keep your finger away from the switch when tightening a drill in the chuck of a live power drill.

Make sure that power tool switches are in the "off" position before plugging in.

Hand Tools

When racking chisels, do not let them dangle with exposed cutting edges.

Before starting an operation, anticipate what is likely to happen if the work should break or shift in the vice, a tool were to slip or jam, or a blade should break.

Fit all files with a handle. If an un-handled file jams for some reason, the pointed tang can be driven into the palm of your hand. Bleeding from such cuts can be difficult to control.

Whatever some manufacturers' illustrations suggest, use a mallet with a chisel. The mallet has a big head, so you can carefully watch the business end of the chisel yet watch the mallet with the corner of your eye. If you miss, or make a glancing blow with a hammer, you can receive a nasty knock on your hand. (*Fig. 13*)

When pulling a mortise chisel out of a mortise, keep your chin out of the way. The chisel can jump out suddenly.

A badly sharpened handsaw will have some teeth that project more than others. These can snag and jump the saw out of the cut, maybe onto your hand.

Beware of metal splinters often left attached to a slotted screw head after a screwdriver has slipped.

FIG. 13

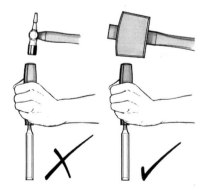

Whenever possible use G cramps with the screws pointing downwards. If they stick upwards, there is a risk to your face.

Never try to catch a falling chisel. Jump your feet apart to avoid a cut.

Techniques

Mind your knee when sawing on a sawing horse. You can catch your leg with the back teeth of a handsaw. (*Fig. 14*)

When hacksawing metal, saw nearly through then
waggle the offcut to break it off. Sawing right through a
piece of metal is likely to lead to a hand crashing onto a
sharp edge.

FIG. 14

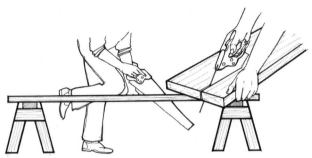

INDEX